A Cage
Called Job

BY

Sherique Dill

Author: /Sherique Dill
Street Address: Nassau, New Providence
Bahamas
www. charisnasimms.wixsite.com/authorsheriquedill

Book Layout ©2017 BookDesignTemplates.com

Ordering Information:
Quantity sales. Special discounts are available on quantity purchases by corporations, associations, and others. For details, contact the author at the address above.

A Cage Called Job/ Sherique Dill
ISBN-13:978-1973978992

CONTENTS

Dedication

I dedicate this book to my loving and supportive husband Jowelle 'Solo' Dill. You have always been my pillar of strength. I would not be where I am today if it was not for our strong union.

To my sons Joden and Jyelle Dill and my expected child, you are my motivation for wanting to achieve more out of life. My objective is to pave the way for you, and to leave a great legacy so that you can be proud to call me your mother.

To my parents Linda and Cyril Simms and my deceased Grandparents Sherwin and Christine Simms, I thank you for your guidance, wisdom and knowledge.

Lastly but importantly, to you the reader, I appreciate you. This book is unsuccessful without your support. This book is to encourage you to believe that you can have ownership and that you're limitless. There is no limit to what The Most High has created you to do. My objective is to positively influence you and I hope that I have done that.

Freedom is not about the size of your cage or power of your wings or non-attachment to a person or a thing. Freedom is about being so truly, madly and deeply attached to your own soul that you can't bear-if only for a moment- a life that doesn't honor it.

—ANDREA BALT

Introduction

Dissatisfaction, frustration, discouragement, stress, unhappiness, pain and low self-esteem; these are the emotions of individuals that are out of place when it comes to their true work.

All of us have great potential, and to reach the highest level of potency, one must be free to decide the direction of his/her destiny. Potential represents untapped strengths, unreleased influence, unused energy, hidden gifts, unexposed success, reserved power, untouched effectiveness, and unrealized discoveries/inventions.

There are things that you can do that you haven't done; there are places you can go that you haven't gone; there are people that you can influence that you haven't yet influenced; there are things that you can see happen in your life that you haven't yet seen; and there are words that you can say that you haven't yet said. These are the possibilities constricted by a job.

Being an employee for your entire life will not truly benefit you or your family; at some point, you should break away from the corporate plantation and become the master of your life. Jobs are sophisticated methods of slavery because they have the ability to control your time and wealth. Time plays an important role in wealth because your level of wealth is determined by exceptional time management (high productivity with time). A job is also a sophisticated method of slavery because slavery was all about having laborers: people to work the cotton field, do house work, etc. The only things different with a job is that you're being paid for labor; you can go home to your family and you have the free will to get another job if you wish. However, it all boils down to you being a paid slave. The scheme still exists. Responsibility belongs to the oppressor.

There is no big difference between the wealthy and the poor, except their mentality. Both groups have the same exact amount of time (24 hours a day). The wealthy choose to maximize on their time.

Many people that have a job find themselves living in poverty—living from pay check to pay check. They are just living to survive and pay bills. In addition, they are only able to provide for themselves because they lack wealth, which causes their generation to suffer.

I'm not totally against jobs; jobs are great starting-off points because of the knowledge and experience that you can gain while being there. My intent is to provoke thought and to influence you to expand your view above just having a job and to let you know that jobs won't lead you towards the path of wealth; having a successful business will.

I value myself and I believe that I'm worth more than what my job can offer me, which is why I am an aspiring entrepreneur. I have decided that I will not live in limitations like many people for the duration of my life.

Wealthy people comprehend what it takes to obtain and maintain financial independence and financial liberation. The majority of people who are not trained to have this type of mentality see their job as their savior, and the result is poverty. Too many people believe (through manipulation) that they have to die to experience heaven or hell. This is sad, because the minority is enjoying heaven on earth while the majority experience hell (poverty).

When most people talk about their jobs, there is an expression of meaninglessness. There is high frustration, and this high frustration signifies that people are aware that they are living below their potential. They are unclear about their life's purpose.

When you discover your life's purpose, you will have the ability to tap into your greatest potential. Your passion will flow like a river. You will be excited to wake up in the morning because you own your work—unlike a job.

There are many people that share my frustrations, and this is why this book exists. My intention is to motivate, and inspire others to rise with me.

I don't regret being in the cage of a job. I have a genuine story that many can relate to—a story that will make a difference in someone's life. One good thing about being in a cage is that once you have been empowered and you have been made free, no one can place you in a cage again; you would rather die than to go back in that cage; that's the power of freedom. If you are unable to mark an area that you are willing to die for, then you don't know what it truly means to be free.

CHAPTER 1

The desire for change

A few years ago, at my job, I sat at my desk and, while performing my recurrent tasks and duties, I contemplated the direction of my life. I felt a great void. It all started in my mind: thoughts of true success. I was unsatisfied and unfulfilled because I kept operating at jobs that didn't stimulate my mind. I had no definite focus in regards to my true work. I was sure of one thing: I knew that I was operating significantly below my potential. I knew that I wanted to make significant contributions to this great planet.

I had so much on the inside of me that I wanted to share. I wanted to engage in things that would give me a higher feeling of self-importance.

I knew that The Most High had chosen me for a specific task; all I needed to do was to find this task and allow The Most High to direct and use me.

I had a vision, and from this vision came my true burning desires—desires that would one day become reality. What are you thinking? You will attract from the universe whatever thoughts you allow to dominate your mind. The moment I became attracted to living a life with meaning, I was aligned with people and avenues that could manifest these thoughts.

I was once a wisher. I made a decision that I would no longer wish I had this, or wish I could do that; for true success doesn't become reality through mere wishes. When you have desires, backed up by belief and passion, you can accomplish anything.

There is a difference between wish and desire. Wishing does not invoke emotions of passion. It is a weak request that is void of determination and persistence.

Desires are much deeper than mere wishes; to desire means to long for, to crave or to become obsessed with a thing. A desire is an extreme obsession that will not allow you to accept failures but see them as temporary defeat.

Get angry

Are you happy with the way things are going? If you are not happy, get angry. There is good anger and bad anger. Good anger motivates and inspires positive changes (a healthy emotion). Bad anger or harmful anger attracts negative energies and could cause you to act foolishly, harming yourself or others (a very unhealthy emotion). So the emotion of anger is not all bad; good anger is needed to achieve success. When you're satisfied with your life, you lose the will to set goals and achieve them. Desires or wanting is what keeps us spiritually and emotionally alive. We don't enjoy life because of the things we need. Who is in love with life because they need to drink water or breathe in oxygen? We love life because of desires and hope. We live because we believe that something greater exist and we want to experience it. This is the essence of life.

Complacency

You don't change things that you are complacent with. Complacency is an enemy to change. If you wake up one day and you feel like something is missing, so much so that you feel empty and sad, then you are at the start of your journey to finding your life's purpose, you are at the beginning stage of change. Showing up at a job every day that you hate is similar to committing suicide. In this case, the suicide is spiritual. It is killing you on the inside.

Getting infuriated with your current situation does not mean that you are ungrateful or unthankful; it fuels your passion for wanting better, for being better. I'm thankful for my job because it has afforded me a comfortable lifestyle; however, my true work is greater than me. Do not ignore these signs. If you ignore these signs and continue to live in dissatisfaction, you will suffer emotionally, spiritually, mentally and physically. It will make you sick.

When exposed to purpose, nothing will fulfill you

My dissatisfactions started out small and inconsistent because I was ignorant of purpose and I didn't know why I felt frustrated. When I became exposed to the concept of purpose the dissatisfactions grew larger and more consistent. I tried to seek new beginnings by moving from one place to the next, hoping to find satisfaction and fulfillment; fortunately, the feelings got worse. I realized that nothing outside of purpose would fulfill me. If you are experiencing this fire, it's not anxiety, it's not a midlife crisis, you are not confused and you are not going crazy; you desire more of life.

Comfortableness delays changes

When you are comfortable, you will have no desire for change. Comfortableness hinders growth. You cannot afford to remain comfortable; you have a generation that is depending on you. You must keep moving and get rid of the spirit of comfortableness. Even when you accomplish something great, you must move on to something greater. There is always something on earth for you to do. You should never get comfortable with the level of your last success. Wealthy people don't get comfortable in all their riches; they're always working, going after every opportunity, seeking to dominant the world. If you want the wealth, you have to adapt this mentality.

I use my anger and frustration as motivation. It is one of the things that drive me towards true success because it increases my desire. There is little that drives me more than coming across situations where I can prove that I'm valuable when others don't believe that I am.

Faith without works is dead

Some people have a positive mind-set and passion, but they lack self-discipline and execution. It is good to be optimistic and see the good in all your situations; however, positive thinking and passion is not enough to win. People think positively, and that is all they do: think and never act. When you get angry at your situation when seeking change, there are other qualities needed in order for your desires to become reality. You must be disciplined and decide that you are going to be the master of your life despite your emotions. You must think big, believe in yourself, set goals, create plans, and backup those plans with persistence, never recognizing failure. You must act on your decisions. There is no genie in a bottle that will magically take you to your success; neither is there a magic button that you can press that will make success appear. You have to think it, believe it and work hard for it.

Timing is vital to change

Even if you're on a job and you're unsatisfied, you must comprehend how vital timing is. You can have a great idea, be knowledgeable, have a high positive energy, and also put in a lot of hard work, but because you moved prematurely (no plans in place), you will experience unnecessary pain and suffering.

Success is a journey. This is why it is crucial to be prepared for life's hurdles. You might not know exactly how you will be tested, but be assured that trials will come.

How will you know the right time? Well, the truth is that there will never be a perfect time to go after your desires. If you keep waiting on that perfect time, you will find every excuse not to pursue your desires. However, a good sign that you are ready to launch out is that you will get a strong feeling of passion. You will have high confidence in yourself, believing that you will accomplish your visions because you have completed your planning. Doors (opportunities) will unbelievably open for you that no one can close; opportunities that you didn't imagine will come your way. You will be fully prepared (financially, mentally, emotionally, spiritually, and physically). Most of all, your source (The Most High) will alert you through divine revelations and insights.

The idea of leaving your job to start your own business is a great feeling. Not only is it a great feeling, but it is a genuine feeling, because no person was born to be a slave. It is a natural desire to be free from the control of others. However, be cautious; don't allow these overwhelming emotions to cause you to leave ahead of your destined time. In addition, jobs are very powerful. Jobs are strongholds. When you leave your job unprepared, at the first sign of defeat you will be ready to throw in the towel because you have no plans. When you decide to leave this cage, you must have clear directions; if not, you will return to it because you did not prepare for the inevitable temporary defeats.

CHAPTER 2

Work your Worth

True worth cannot be determined until potential is discovered. Untapped potency equals uncalculated worth. No one on this planet can afford to compensate you for your potential. You are the only person that has the ability to compensate yourself justly because only you can release your potential. This is why your environment is vital; your environment will either hide your potential or unleash it.

The Creator knows the extent of your potential. Your carnal mind is unable to calculate your highest potential. In order for this divine insight to flow through you, you must maintain your relationship and become one with The Most High. Then, and only then, will your highest potential be maximized. This is when you reach your level of divinity.

Your worth is immeasurable because your DNA carries experiences and capabilities from your genetic descendants and ancestors. You are a divine god/goddess operating in a physical form (body). In addition, your origins precede the sun, moon and stars because you are made in the image and likeness of The Most High. If you are made in the image and likeness of The Most High, you have the ability to operate the way The Most High operates. The measurement of your potential is like a deep, dark, endless ocean.

Never assume that people should know your value

It is your responsibility to display your potential so that others can appreciate your value. Don't assume that people should automatically value you. You have to display what you are and what you can do so that you are not only valuable to yourself but you become valuable to others. It's important for people to know your worth because your gifts/potencies are given to you so that you can serve others. Your gifts/potent areas have no effectiveness if you don't share them.

This is why people are mistreated and degraded at their jobs. They are not given the opportunity to display what makes them valuable because they are limited by job descriptions, duties and assignments.

In addition, people hold in high esteem those that have something to offer. So allowing people to see your value is not about you trying to please them; it is deeper than that. The reality is that you have to give something valuable if you want to get something valuable in return. If you want a great life, you have to do great things. There is no such thing as getting something for nothing. This is not how the universe operates. Freedom is not free. There's a price tag (sacrifices) attached to freedom. This is why people who like to receive but refuse to give don't achieve true success.

Greater value equals greater respect

You must learn how to work your worth because when people perceive you as a valuable person, they will be cautious of how they act with you because they fear losing you. When your work appears valuable, people will allow you to influence them.

Even if they envy you, they will follow you. They will keep you close to them because you have something that they need. There is something on the inside of you that the planet needs. This will make you a powerful person because the high demand for your gifts/potencies will take you before kings and queens.

Low self confidence in the Corporate World

In the corporate world, there are many employees that suffer from low self-confidence. They are victims of the corporate prostitutes (high-ranking employees that seek to control others). I call them corporate prostitutes because they carry out the order of the corporate system. This is why I had to include Chapter 3 (The Power of Environments) in this book. Not knowing who you are in the corporate world is dangerous to your self-confidence because this is where you spend most of your time. If you allow this environment to determine your worth, you will end up feeling useless and unimportant. Instead of feeling like a king or queen, you will end up feeling like a slave. In the corporate world, you are mostly judged by your job status. Those employees that have the lower positions are often looked down on. The employees with lower positions are not seen as valuable. Most of the higher-ranking employees are arrogant, and they don't believe that they can learn from the employees with lower positions. They don't believe that the employees in lower positions can make valuable contributions. This is reality, and it probably won't change because this is the mentality that the corporate world breeds. The corporate system is designed to promote segregation. It is designed to treat one group of people (in a high position) better than the other group. It is designed to keep control over the masses and damage their self-confidence so that they will not rise. You have to know who you are. You must know your value. You must believe in yourself and not be distracted by job status. Your job status has nothing to do with your capabilities, and it certainly has nothing to do with your self-worth. This is why most employees don't desire more out of life, because their self-confidence is damaged while being on their job and they don't believe that they deserve anything better. A low self-confidence is one of the main reasons why some people don't love their job. They feel unappreciated, unimportant and unrecognized, so they perform average or below average just to get a pay check.

Materialism can never replace self-worth

Many people seek satisfaction through materialism. Trying to appear valuable with materialism is a false perception of self-worth. Many employees tie their self-worth to their job status. This is why they feel lifeless or empty when they can no longer be at their job. In addition, this is why many employees have a low self-esteem, because they depend on their job to make them feel good about themselves. When they are fired or let go from their jobs, they are depressed. People chase after money instead of chasing after their life's purpose. Many people take care of themselves externally, but internally they are hurting and they are unfulfilled. If you believe that materialism can replace self-worth, you will continue to live in bondage. It is a distraction. When you can be manipulated into believing that materialism is more valuable than true self-worth, you are in trouble.

Contributing to other people's success

At a job, you normally spend most of your critical hours building someone else's value, worth and financial wealth. What you are is a babysitter; you are babysitting other people's visions. If you can do this for other people, you are capable of doing it for yourself; you can be the full parent of your own vision instead of babysitting and falling in love with other people's visions. The same energy that drives you to slave for someone else can drive you towards ownership. If you don't have your own dreams and visions, those that do will hire you to turn their dreams and visions into reality. This happens a lot with educated students; they invest their time, acquire extensive knowledge, inherit large debts, and then look for a job.

Worth determined in the corporate world

Employers determine an employee's worth in the corporate world. However, when your employer is aware of your worth, you can demand your income and benefits.

When you are looking for a job, the first thing you would normally do is prepare a resume. What is a resume? This important document will give your employer details of your skills, experiences, previous jobs, tasks and duties you performed, career objectives, etc. Therefore, this document is like a guide, and it will help them determine if you will be valuable to their organization. Your objective when applying for a job is to beguile (captivate, entice) your employer so that they can see how you will benefit their organization. Therefore, this process has little to do with you. Employers will determine your worth by determining your wages, deciding how much of your time they want and whether you are deserving of a promotion, sick benefits and vacation leave.

When you interact with people, they can only determine how valuable you are to them. They have their own perception of what you are worth (which is their right); however, their perception can be controlled by you because you are the only person that can lessen your value or increase it. The Most High has already made you to be the magnificent being that you are. Therefore, you have to set your standard; you have to put on display what you are worth. Do not allow people to launch their false perceptions of who you really are. People will always be willing to give their opinions about you; however, don't allow their opinion to become facts. If you don't tap into your potent areas and display true worth, others will be happy to determine and perceive your worth, and most likely it will not be in your favor. It is up to you to determine whether you will be known as a replaceable or irreplaceable being. Only your true work can make you irreplaceable. Every skill known to us can be replaced. No one can replace you in an area that you were born to operate in. They can't replace your passion and your natural connection to that area. Personal attributes are irreplaceable. After you are gone, they can fill the vacancy with another person; however, that person will bring their own uniqueness to that area.

Take into consideration the effect of your job. Is it causing you to bloom like a beautiful flower or is it like a blood-sucking vampire, sucking the positive life force out of you, making you feel hopeless? No job should have that power over you.

CHAPTER 3

The Power of Environments

You are your environments. Your environments or surroundings are not just a location or atmosphere; your environments have a deep connection to your mental state. Your thoughts, your actions, your mannerism, your beliefs, your standards and all the things that contribute to your character were all built from your environments.

The social environment is extremely powerful. Social environments form patterns and behaviors. Therefore, social environments influence individuals. This environment impacts families, communities, societies, and nations because it is the point of interaction.

Some examples of social environments are: home (family) environments, educational environments, recreational environments, church environments, job environments and social media.

PART 1

Family environments

The first environment that will influence you is your family. In this environment, you will learn how to survive on earth from the information of your parents. When you existed in your mother's womb, she was your first human interaction. The first thing you heard was the sound of her heartbeat and her voice. You learned language by listening to her voice. You fed off of her emotions, and she was the first love of your life.

Your family will teach you right from wrong, and their perceptions of life will set the basis of your values, standards, beliefs, and morals. These attributes will form your character, and they will determine how you make decisions in every aspect of life. The family environment, particularly parents, has a major influence when it comes to the destiny of their children. This is why at an early age parents must pay close attention to their children's high potentials and encourage them to fulfill their life's purpose. Parents should never encourage their children to 'just get a job,' so to speak. When you do that, you are no better than the house slave that had a responsibility to keep the other slaves in line and obey their masters. You are not participating towards their physical bondage; you are participating towards their mental bondage, which contributes to economic and financial bondage. The mentality or state of mind of your children is a reflection of your state of mind.

The family environment is also the most powerful social environment because a great family births a great nation. The social ills that we are experiencing today are due to the downfall of families. We must continue to protect this most sacred environment, and parents must comprehend their importance and that they have a responsibility that is greater than them.

Job Environments

Most people desire jobs at the age of maturity because they have been trained from tender ages to believe that jobs are financial saviors. In Chapter 13, I discuss how this mentality can be transformed by building a family empire (business).

The type of jobs that you are attracted to actually reflect what's on the inside of you. This is why, in Chapter 2, I spoke about worth. In Chapter 1, I spoke about the desire for change. If you are growing and developing, you will have the desire to attract a higher standard. You can only attract to you what you are, and the universe will give back to you, what you give to the universe. If you think great, you give great and you act great, then you are great. If you think you are not worthy, you lack confidence, you are slothful and you refuse to do things of importance and meaning, then this is what you will continue to attract to you; you will get what you deserve.

Most people interact with the greatest amount of people at their jobs. This is where you spend your most valuable hours. Your most valuable hours are between 8 am–6 pm depending on your demographics. This is basically the period where you would have the most sunlight.

You must pay close attention to this social environment. You must be conscious of the energies it forms. When you interact with people, you are interacting with different personalities, attitudes, values, morals, mentalities, principles, characters and beliefs. One must comprehend the power of the human brain; it feeds off of energy and can transmit energy. Energy can be positive or negative. Here are some examples of how to determine negative social environments:

No growth and development

If you have no desire for growth and development, then you will automatically be attracted to a job that has no ability to promote growth and development in your life. This explains the satisfaction of an individual that has been employed with a company performing the same task and duties for a long period of time. In Chapter 6, I will explain how having a job is different from your work. Your job duties and tasks are prearranged; they are recurrent and ceremonial. Your work will always surprise you and give you unexpected results, which will cause you to grow and develop because you are being exposed to new areas and you are tapping into your deep ocean of endless possibilities.

The misalignment of your environment will   prevent your growth and development. It will cause you to be unfruitful and unproductive. Your environments have an intimate connection to your purpose. In Chapter 8, I will explain how to benefit from having a temporary job status.

People pay little attention to growth. We are not that different from plants; just how we expect plants to grow from a seed into a tree that produces fruit, we are to grow physically, emotionally, mentally and spiritually. We too should produce fruits.

For example, you may have the desire to grow your own sweet peppers. So what do you do? You would first obtain the seed, and then you would do all the necessary things needed for the seed to produce fruit. You will take care in watering the plant, and you will ensure it gets the proper amount of sunlight. You realize that in order for the tree to produce fruit you must place it in the right environment. So why do you pay so much attention to the plant's environment and think so little of your own environment? If you evaluate your life and find that you are not growing as an individual, you are in disagreement with nature. Growth is a natural divine order.

No mentorship

You should be able to identify someone in your environment as your mentor. If you don't have someone to inspire you or influence you to make positive decisions, you are in the wrong environment.

Harmful criticism

People often say that words cannot harm you. Words will harm you; words are powerful. Many times you are not conscious of the impact they have on your life until things start to manifest. Then you're left wondering where it came from. You must be very careful of who you allow into your space. This includes friends and sometimes family. While it may have been innocent, there are a lot of people that suffer from low self-confidence issues because of things said to them through negative opinions and negative criticism. Those negative opinions and negative criticisms are trapped within your subconscious mind, reminding you every day that you aren't good enough. So you create your reality from other people's negativity. Criticisms without solutions are harmful. Pay no attention to criticism that is intended to damage your self-confidence. Many people that enter your environment will have no ability to promote growth and development in your life. They only care about highlighting your weaknesses, and they have no intention to show you how to turn your weaknesses into strength. Therefore, take notice of who you put confidence in; only allow people into your council that are in alignment with your purpose and would never jeopardize you or it.

A bird in a cage

A person who is in the wrong environment will feel like a bird trapped in a cage. Birds that are free to explore and to fulfill their reason for existence are more favorable by nature. It's a fact that birds that are kept in cages expire long before birds that are not. When you put a bird in a cage, you are putting a limit on the bird. The bird can only do what the cage allows it to do. If you put a bird into a cage before it has the opportunity to test its wings (fly) the bird will not know or experience the joy and fulfillment of flying. In addition, the bird will be operating below its potential because someone interrupted with nature and removed it from its natural environment. Therefore, at large, Mother Nature loses because purpose isn't being fulfilled.

There are some people that will say that their surroundings don't determine how they act; however, they are ignorant of the laws of attraction and they don't know the power of the subconscious mind. The subconscious mind never ceases to take in information. This means that negativity can creep into your mind without your conscious permission.

You never want to have your own business one day because at your job you are not associating with business-minded people. You are frustrated and miserable at your job because your co-workers are always frustrated and miserable, passing that emotion onto you. You are afraid to take risks because everyone else around you is afraid to take risks. You are not interested in discovering your gifts because the people around you have not discovered theirs.

You must guard the windows to your soul. Pay close attention to the things that you see, hear, taste and touch, because these things have the ability to affect your judgments and your ability to make good decisions.

Light doesn't agree with darkness

If you are a positive person, you will find yourself not fitting into your negative environment; which is a good thing because you should not fit in; you should always stand out. You will not fit in because your mind-set is not in alignment with your co-worker's mind-set. Mentally and spiritually, you are on different levels, so they will start to accuse you of being unfriendly or unsociable. It's not that you are unfriendly; you have discerned their negativity and you don't want negativity to infect you. Negativity is a contagious disease: easy to catch but hard to get rid of.

Unhealthy Job environments will affect family life and personal health

When you are working in an unhealthy job environment, eventually the negative energy will follow you home. This creates a big problem because the most important people in your life—your spouse (if married) and your children—will be in jeopardy. This negative energy will affect your personal health. Going into an environment every day that makes you unhappy is not the will of The Most High. The will of The Most High is for you to work in peace and harmony. When you work in a peaceful and harmonious environment you can perform at your highest frequency.

PART 2

The Right Job Environments

Your right environment is your Garden of Eden. In the scriptures, the Garden of Eden was where Adam and Eve were created and existed.

Everything that they needed was in the Garden of Eden (food, shelter, wealth, resources, etc.). This clearly shows that if you are operating outside of your Garden of Eden, you will be in lack. Importantly, in this garden, just how The Most High would communicate with Adam and Eve, The Most High will communicate with you. Plainly, if you are not in your Garden of Eden (right environment) there will be a blockage in regards to communication between you and The Most High. If you are having challenges receiving spiritual revelations and insights from The Most High, check your location. Your Garden of Eden is your natural environment. This garden is your lifeline; it will nourish you, sustain you, replenish you, rejuvenate you, and fulfill you. Everything that you need to survive on earth is found within your Garden of Eden.

Only you will know what environments are right for you. These environments will pull out your great potentials and allow you to flow effortlessly. Right environments will always connect you to your purpose and a higher meaning for your life. Your right environment is like a battery. When you feel down and exhausted from the struggles of life and you feel like your strength is drained, right environments will charge you up. They are your generator; they generate positive energy and power.

Excited to wake up in the mornings

When you are in the right environment, you will wake up in the morning excited to work. Going to work will introduce you to fulfillment and happiness. Unfortunately, this is not the case for many people because they aren't in love with their jobs. You should feel like a kid on Christmas morning—a kid that overflows with anticipation because he/she know that this day comes with great expectations. Just how a kid is excited to receive their gifts on Christmas and proud to show it to their friends and loved ones, you should be excited to discover and display your gifts and eager to share them with humanity.

Growth and development

Right environments are conducive for growth and development. The energy that exists in these environments will be so powerful that you will have self-motivation, a high self-esteem, persistence, confidence, strength, courage, will, exuberance, and so many positive traits. Your life will have meaning; you will have a sense of value and high self-importance in this environment. You will have a sense of fulfillment because you have permission to display your gifts; you are saturated with passion and you are working (walking in purpose). You will be learning new things about yourself.

When you are in the right environment, it will surprise you. Right environments will produce unexpected value.

Responsibility and accountability

Right environments inspire responsibility and accountability. These environments will promote a strong energy where you will want to have something you can pass down to your children, something worth fighting for, something that you would die for. This is a sign that will assure you that you are in your Garden of Eden.

I know what it feels like to be outside of my Garden of Eden. I was outside of my right environment for a long time, and it affected me. It affected my self-esteem and confidence. When you see others excelling in their particular field, it can make you feel left out, believing that The Most High did not bless you with gifts. It can make you feel like a failure and make you feel invaluable. However, that feeling is a deception. You have something on the inside of you that you were born to do. You have your area of potency. All you need is realignment: get in the right environment. The same energy that you may use to envy others can be directed towards finding your strengths and passions.

How will you discover your passion for teaching if you work in an environment that has no connection to teaching? How will you discover your passion for writing if you are in an environment where you are not required to write? How will you know that you are potent when it comes to motivation and inspiration if you don't have the ability to interact with people that need to be inspired or motivated?

Years ago, and still today, I would come into contact with people that would assume that I was a professional teacher. I would smile and wonder why people would often ask me that. I didn't have the desire to pursue a teaching career, so I paid it no attention. The last thing I could have seen myself doing was standing in a classroom teaching. Later on, for an unknown reason, I had a desire to transfer into a school. I was obedient to this desire. My professional area of training is in finance and accounting, which I have done for years. So transferring into a school took me out of my field. I had many doubts because I felt out of place and I knew that I was working far below my potential. Many times I wanted to return to what I did best. However, little that I know, it was a prophecy over my life. Those people were unconscious messengers of The Most High. I am not a trained teacher in the classroom, but I am a divine educator, educating people through my books and with words of wisdom inspired by The Most High. My platform is bigger than a classroom because I have the ability to educate globally. In addition, my words will live beyond my physical body. In death, my ability to educate, motivate and inspire will exist.

This environment came with a special reason, a reason that was bigger than me and bigger than what I wanted. Working in a school, interacting with students and others, birthed the desire for mentoring and coaching. I saw the challenges and I felt a strong burden and responsibility to pass on information for the greater good of this generation and future generations. This is the power of environments. It will cause you to discover the hidden potential and the hidden passions that are needed to be at one with your true work. What if I had not been obedient? I would have missed opportunities. I'm aware that it is a temporary status, because the level that The

Most High will take me to will require freedom. I must have control over my time and wealth.

You are accountable for the environments you allow yourself to be a part of. It is your responsibility to pull the potencies out of you, and if you feel as if the environments that you're in are responsible for your hidden potentials, then you must make the right decisions.

Becoming one with nature

Being in the right environment will cause you to accept and love who you are. You must accept who you are and believe that you are unique and not conform or compromise for the love and acceptance of others.

If your job environment forces a lifestyle on you that is against your beliefs and standards or does not promote or encourage you to be who you are, that is not a good place to be. When you break away from the illusions and things promoted by the world that appears to be real but so untrue and harmful, you will begin to rise. Your mentality about life will start to change. Nature has a way of doing this. Accepting you as unique and original has a lot to do with your success.

Reward and appreciation

When you are in the right work environment, people will reward you, appreciate you and recognize you for your hard work. In this environment, unity with your colleagues and leaders will exist. In addition, the environment will be family oriented: a close bond. Trust, loyalty and commitment will be in this environment.

Guardian angels

All right environments have guardian angels. These individuals will keep you on the right path; they are there to guide you to your destiny of purpose. They will bring insight, revelations and wisdom. The Most High will also place them within your wrong environment if needed so that you can be inspired to leave. Guardian angels come to you in so many different forms. Most people believe that guardian angels are invisible beings. Guardian angels can come in physical form, or through revelations and divine inspirations.

CHAPTER 4

Job Slaves

When you go to your job, you do what is required of you by your employer and you are paid for that labor. When you are incapable of laboring, your income will stop. This means that you have no leverage. If you are satisfied with the concept of 'Labor once, paid once', you have the job mentality. You can either have a job mentality or an ownership mentality. People that have the ownership mentality have the desire to work with people, rather than labor for people.

Who is a job slave?

Jobs slaves are complacent laboring for others until they reach the corporate mandatory age of retirement. Job slaves believe that the only way to success is through the almighty job, and they have no desire to build a family empire. Job slaves negotiate with poverty. They accept the position that they're in and do absolutely nothing to change it. Well, they do one thing: they complain. Job slaves have wishes; they wish they could have a better life, but those wishes never turn into reality. They are lazy when it comes to knowledge, and they have no desire to unleash their potential. They stay within their small cage. Job slaves have no clarity or focus; they are void of direction. They are unable to make definitive decisions. Their indecisiveness causes them to frequently blame others. They have no idea what they want to become, and they have no desire to own things. Job slaves strive to obtain money (currency) rather than wealth.

Job slaves don't invest

People that are free of the job mentality seek to invest in opportunities that will pay them long term. Job slaves believe that they have reached a level of success because they have funds saved in the bank and they would rarely invest it. They have labored so hard for their income, and risking it through investment is not an option for them. This is why their wealth grows slowly. In addition, job slaves are not savvy when it comes to making great business decisions.

Job slaves don't maximize their time

The job mentality creates this illusion that work should only be through the day, hence the terms *day job* and *nine to five*. This mind-set is crippling, and it is responsible for the poverty of many. The concept of laboring 40 hours a week was made popular by Henry Ford. Henry Ford wanted to attract workers from other companies by giving them less hours a week. Laboring 40 hours a week will not get you to your destination of success. You must get into your mind that you won't experience true wealth laboring for others, so when you come from your day job, you must invest the remainder of your time into your work so that you can build your own wealth. When you rise above the job mentality, your work is morning, day and night. Your work becomes consistent. It becomes a part of you. Job slaves believe that the time spent at their job is a full day's work, and they would not use the remainder of their time to plan a great future. They have a problem staying up some late nights to work on their own plan for success because they are burned out from their master's job. In addition, they lack self-discipline.

Job slaves are satisfied with what their jobs offer them because they are too lazy to do more than what they are doing. They are afraid to tap into their area of potency. They love to sleep more than they love to work. When they are not sleeping, they use their free time watching the television, partying, gossiping and doing idle work. Nothing is wrong with watching the television occasionally, if you are watching things that contribute to your productivity. If you are watching shows or movies that are for pure entertainment and it has no ability to uplift you, you are being idle and you are saturating your brain with foolishness. Those that are free of the job mentality have to force themselves to go to sleep because their passion for greatness is so big that it stimulates them and they barely notice the time. People that are free of the job mentality sleep because they have to, not because they want to. There are too many great things going on inside their minds; therefore, sleeping is not their best friend; it is perceived as an enemy. Although getting the proper rest is required, people that are truly working feel as if they need to maximize every second of their time.

People that are truly working feel as if time goes by too quickly. Job slaves often feel as if time is moving too slow because they are not maximizing their potential. Time only moves slow for people that are unproductive. If you are at your day job doing the same recurrent duties that drain your energy, time will move slowly for you. Why? Because you are doing nothing! You might be physically laboring, but time spent on things other than your true meaning for life is considered to be nothing. It means nothing in the eyes of the Creator. If an iron doesn't heat, even though the physical structure is in good standing, to the customer the iron does nothing; it is no good. The customer will then dispose of the product because it doesn't have the ability to fulfill its manufacturing purpose.

Jobs slaves miss the big picture

Job slaves don't connect their jobs to cages because they miss the big picture. While being satisfied at your job is important, you must also consider two precious commodities: time and wealth. If you are not in control of your time and your ability to create wealth for your family, you are still enslaved. Job slaves don't see their job as cages because they are selfish; they are satisfied with duties and assignments instead of building a generational empire. It is possible to be at a job and be satisfied; however, you will still be under limitations. If you love to cook and you are a chef, have the will to open up your own restaurant in the future. If you are a DJ and you love music, be determined to own your radio station in the future. If you love fashion, be determined to open up a clothing/shoe store in the future. Have the will to be your own master. You are not in control when you labor for others; you have to abide by their rules and policies.

Job slaves don't cherish their young days

Your youthful days are the most crucial period of life. If you take advantage of this period it will bring you tremendous success in the future, if not, it will cause you tremendous defeat. This period is when most people make critical mistakes. They make critical mistakes at this age because they lack wisdom, decisiveness, experience, and knowledge. In addition, they are too hasty to explore the dark areas of life. At this stage, life is all about fun and pleasure, and they realize their mistakes much later. They realize it at a time when they do not have the vibrancy, passion and fire to accomplish their aspirations—a time that is often too late.

This behavior places them in the category of dreamers. Dreamers sit down and fantasize about their goals and never accomplish them in their lifetime because they have wasted their youthful days (these are the job slaves).

Spend your young days sowing good seeds so that when you become older, there is no need to worry about life. This period should be the time when you reap the harvest of what you have sowed in your youthful days. This is reality; you will reap what you sow. If you waste time when you are young, being idle, being caught up with negative energies; you will reap the benefit of it when you become older. You will die poor. If you sow seeds of positivity, discovering your true purpose in life, working towards financial independence and liberation, serving others with your gifts, investing time acquiring knowledge, spending time with family, etc., you will reap this harvest; you can ease through your older days because you executed wisdom.

A time of reflection

I contemplated my life. I have made a decision to not sit on someone's job for the rest of my youthful life, wishing or dreaming of the wonderful things I could or should have done. I want to be able to look back and say, "Wow, I did that", or feel a high sense of accomplishment. When I am approaching expiration, I will have no need to feel deep sorrow (sorrow only to leave love ones behind) because I would have lived a life worth living. I'm not going to achieve my desire in a cage; therefore, I have no other choice but to rise above the job mentality.

Job slaves don't believe in unity

Job slaves don't comprehend that unity is power. They don't comprehend that on a job there is no need for hate and envy, that there should be a spirit of peace, love and togetherness. A job should not be a place of competiveness; a job should be a place of learning, a place where people can strive to reach a common goal through unity. Free-minded individuals are not jealous or envious; they are happy to see others excel, and while they are happy, they will discover more about themselves so that they will be empowered.

Many employers don't promote the spirit of love and true relationships at their organizations because they fear unity. When you get along with your co-worker in a friendly matter, you get negative reactions; as if you are not allowed to be friends. This was also popular during the slavery era. The oppressors saw that the slaves would be a greater threat to them being unified. This is why they came up with a plan to separate them. They separated them by having house slaves and field slaves. The house slaves got much better treatment than the field slaves did; they had privileges. So this bred hatred, an attitude that one group was better than the next, forgetting that they were one. Another method of separation was to dilute the skin color, which brought about confusion. Methods of division still exist today; they are just craftier.

Job slaves are ignorant of true work

You can explain extensively how important it is to work your purpose, and job slaves won't comprehend the concept. They don't have the ability to comprehend that in order to call something your true work it must be in alignment with purpose. People mostly care about the necessities of life. Things such as food, clothes, shelter, basic education, paying their bills and recreation. They don't see the value of making their contribution to humanity with their gifts.

Job slaves create more job slaves: their children

Job slaves consciously or unconsciously don't care about the future of their children, so they train their kids to adapt the job mentality. People are not born with the job mentality. This mentality is learned.

Parents with the job mentality would spend their life earnings or last dollar on their children's college education, then encourage them to settle for a job as opposed to building their own empire. This is the most dangerous effect of having the job mentality because it is transferred through generations, affecting the economic power of self and kind.

Job slaves are against mentoring

Globally, in the corporate world, you would discover that people despise mentoring, especially in regards to the younger generation. The spirit of selfishness highly exists in job environments. Job slaves often think about them: how they can progress, how they can make a bigger salary to feed their family and how they can obtain status at their job. Every action is to promote them and it is never to benefit others for the greater good. This mentality creates an illusion where people actually feel as if they will have their job forever. They are insecure, so they will never pass on the knowledge because they fear that others will outshine them. Some people reach their point of retirement, yet still hate to train another person; they would rather pass the information on to the grave. This is not love for your organization; this is hate, because if you love the organization you labor for, you will take delight in making sure the organization can operate whether you are there or not. People that are free of the job mentality comprehend that it is their duty to mentor the younger generation, or to mentor any individual, because by doing so you are acting in preservation of humanity. It is your due diligence to humanity; we are here to accumulate information and then pass it on to those who will continue to contribute to this planet. People shouldn't hoard information; when you expire, you should expire empty. The planet shouldn't lose when you expire. If you are an expert, successful in a field, it is your due diligence to mentor someone that is weak in the area you are an expert in. It is a privilege to be a mentor to someone, and it is the most rewarding thing that you can ever do in your life. A lot of people despise mentorship because they want everything to just be about them. Once they make it, they are satisfied. People need to get rid of this mentality and realize that it is also important to contribute to the growth and development of others. It makes no sense for you to be successful, leaving others behind in poverty if you can help, because you would only have the burden of providing for them. It makes more sense to train them so that they can take care of themselves. If I'm successful and you're successful, you have no need to steal from me, envy me or depend on me. We as a people must learn how to make the wealth common by sharing in any way we can.

Where would we be if our ancestors had the hoarder mentality? We have knowledge and we can accomplish success because the people who existed before us passed on information. They left information (divine revelations, spiritual insights, written communications, etc.) to ensure our survival. What would happen if they were greedy and selfish like many of the people today? If they were greedy and selfish, most of us would still be trying to figure out what plants cure certain diseases, how to build, the nature of animals, etc. We can now be successful and rely on the knowledge and wisdom of our descendants and ancestors. Therefore, we must return to this mentality.

Job slaves see their employers as a boss

The title 'boss' has deep meanings, and the spirit behind it is oppressive. This word indicates that the person you are referring to at your job is supreme. You should refer to the person who has responsibility over you at your job as a leader, manager or supervisor. Work leaders, managers or supervisors have the responsibility of directing staff to reach the desired goals of the organization and at the same time helping them to grow and develop. In Chapter 12, I will further discuss abuse of leadership.

The word 'boss' comes from the Dutch word '*baas*,' which historically means 'master.' Every time you use this word, you are unconsciously giving that person power over your life; you are announcing them as master and lord of your life in the workplace and that you will comply with their every command. You are saying to them that their word and action is law. You are declaring and accepting your inferiority to them.

Many can attest that they have worked under some bosses that act like slave masters, where you have no freedom of speech and you must do what you're told to do and ask no questions. The startling thing to me is that the so called bosses that look just like you, that came from the same background as you and that endured the same struggles as you are the ones that are the cruelest. They have forgotten where they came from.

Making a word more convenient or appropriate doesn't change the spirit or the intention of it. Every time you use this word, you are releasing an amount of fear into your life. This is why you're afraid to tell your employer how you feel or question their wrongful actions. You're afraid that your master will take away your income. You're unconsciously making yourself inferior. This word is spiritually rooted and grounded by evil. Your supervisors/managers are leaders;

they are not masters. They are not superior to you; you are both equal and you have to take on this mentality.

Leaders lead you to freedom, bosses/masters take you back to slavery (Sherique Dill

Leaders have a divine responsibility to lead you and guide you for the accomplishment of a goal, not to mistreat and abuse you to make up for their low self-esteem. Most of these people that abuse their power have no control over their own lives, and the only thing that makes them feel good about themselves is to control and dominate others. Being able to control and manipulate other people makes them feel worthy and it makes their life exciting because if you subtract their seat of power, they really have nothing.

CHAPTER 5

Rising Above the Job Mentality

Many are called to build a family empire, but only a few will be successful. Some people don't have the qualities and skills to build a successful business. This in no way means that it is impossible for them; it means that those who don't have the qualities and skills must do more work and become knowledgeable on how to run a successful business. They have to work harder on themselves by building their character. The reality is that only a few people are willing to put in the hard work, and this is why more people have jobs and less people have businesses.

When you decide to open a business, you must do it for the right reasons. You shouldn't want to open a business only because you hate your job or you hate working for people. You shouldn't want to open a business only because it's an opportunity to make more money. You shouldn't want to open a business only because you don't like working with other people. You shouldn't want to open a business only because you don't like having a manager telling you what to do at your job. These are not well-founded reasons. You should open a business because nothing makes you happier than being able to solve other people's problems. This is the reason why we exist. You should see your business as a solution, not an escape route. You should be connected to it and it should match your passions and interests.

Having a job is a much easier route for income than owning a business because all you have to do is trade skills and time. When you have a business you have to rely on customers to purchase your products or services. Therefore, if no one comes to your business to purchase your product or service, you will have no income. Owning a successful business calls for great qualities and certainly a great mind-set. It is not a walk in the park. The road will not be easy.

You must go into it with the mind-set 'The greater the risk, the greater the reward.' You must comprehend that failure will work out for the good. Those who seek to become successful business owners must transform from a 'mediocre employee mind-set' to an 'entrepreneurial mind-set.' In a nutshell, it's a transformation from dependence to independence, and it's worth the pain and suffering.

Here are some ways owning a business is different from being an employee:

When you are an employee, you can be irresponsible and indecisive, expecting your co-workers to pick up the slack when it comes to your responsibility. When you are in business, you won't be able to pass the buck; the success of your business will depend heavily on your qualities and abilities. You are the master mind behind it all; you are the problem solver and you are the decision maker. You will have to find ways to pull the money from your potential customer's pocket.

When you are an employee, you don't really need planning skills because most things are already planned and designed for you to do. You are basically just the executor. In a business, planning is crucial. You must have a business plan because nobody is going to direct you, and if you fail, failure will be your responsibility. Unlike a job, where there is strong teamwork, you will bear the heavy burden, many times having to do things by yourself. When you have a business, short- and long-term goals must be implemented, which means that you must be prudent.

When you are employed, you are given duties and assignments. You are directed on what to do. Basically, you are following procedures. As a business owner, you must have the capability of initiating self-motivation. There is no one there to direct you; you are the chief. You must direct yourself and make things happen. There is no magic button for success. You must believe in yourself, motivate yourself, and create opportunities for yourself. In a business, you are the lion in the jungle. The zookeeper will not bring food and water to your cage, because you are free. You have to go and hunt for your food; you are independent, responsible and accountable for your destiny.

You must comprehend that when you have a business, consistency is key. You are a brand; people come to you for a unique experience, so you have to remain loyal to maintain their trust in you. Therefore, this requires discipline. When you are an employee, this is rarely important because most employees only care about receiving their wages. They don't really have the passion and commitment because they will still be paid, even if the customer is not happy. This is unacceptable in a business because your level of success depends heavily on how you treat your customers. This is about your reputation, and if your clients are unsatisfied, you will lose them. There is no safety net in a business, like on a job.

When you have a business, program your mind to forget about good benefits such as vacation, maternity leave, compassionate leave, bonuses and sick leave. When you reach the level of entrepreneurship, you can enjoy such privileges, but starting out, you have to work extra hard to get your business to the level where you can relax in the future.

When you have a business, you are capable of hiring your weakness. They will be your professional master mind advisors. So help is always accessible because you are paying for it. This is one of the major reasons why business owners fail. They don't stay in the council of bright minds. They don't comprehend that their mind absorbs energy from the people they are around. Hence the term "Great minds think alike." If you hang around intelligent people, you have no other choice but to be intelligent. If you hang around master minds, you have no other choice but to become a master mind yourself. However, on a job, most co-workers hoard information, so that they can get full credit from their boss. This is why many entry-level employees are unable to rise to higher positions; nobody wants to genuinely train them.

Self-employment vs. Entrepreneurship

Many people believe that because they own a business that they are entrepreneurs. This is a severe misconception, and it is the reason why many self-employers never rise to the level of entrepreneurship. Self-employment and entrepreneurship are not synonymous. The difference between self-employment and entrepreneurship is freedom. There is little to no freedom in self-employment because you are the business. With self-employment, you employ yourself. You can determine your income, but you are not in control of your time. In addition, you won't have that much leverage when it comes to wealth because there is only so much that you can do.

As a self-employed business owner, you put in more time at your business than you would if someone employed you. This is reality, and it is a step that self-employers shouldn't ignore. Many self-employed business owners become burned out and exhausted because they are unable to manage this step. Self-employment can be very risky because it provides little guarantee. Some days you can make money and some days you may not make anything. When you're self-employed, basically you're still on a job, you just happen to be the CEO.

In addition, with self-employment, if you are sick, become disabled or need a vacation, your finances will stop. Self-employed business owners become depressed and stressed because they can't afford to take a break; they are constantly going and thinking about their bills. This is not financial freedom or independence. However, self-employment is the first step to wealth. Most businesses start at this level, then grow over time.

Here is an example of the steps to financial freedom:

Apprentice/Student→Employee→Self-
Employer→Manager (hiring people) →Owner (don't
have to work) → Investor (shares, businesses, real
estate's etc.)→ Entrepreneur.

Entrepreneurs have an entrepreneurial system that allows
them the freedom they desire to do the things they enjoy. The
business/businesses operate without them; they are not the
business. Entrepreneurs hire managers to supervise the
business and they have staff. It's not the size of the business
that determines entrepreneurship; it's the system/structure.

Entrepreneurs make money from investments such as
equities and bonds, purchasing other businesses (mergers and
acquisitions), passive income, etc., which can soundly secure
them and cause them to reach the level of financial
independence and freedom. Entrepreneurs don't work hard
for money; they have a system where money works for them
and it creates wealth continuously. Another great thing about
entrepreneurs is that because they are properly structured and
make investments, they can contribute to the community,
which makes them philanthropists. This is one of the most
rewarding aspects of being an entrepreneur: knowing that
you're in the position financially to help others. So while
self-employment is the first step towards financial freedom
and independence, it's important not to stay there;
entrepreneurship is the ultimate goal.

Freedom of time

Freedom of time is also a great aspect of entrepreneurship.
Entrepreneurship allows you the freedom to do multiple

things that are meaningful to you. When you reach this level, you don't have to limit yourself to one business or one area of calling, but you can spread your wings. As divine beings, there are so many ways that we can have influence and we should enjoy life to the fullest. Some people have multiple gifts; they can open a lucrative business that they love and that will secure them financially, and when they reach the level of entrepreneurship, they can be free to engage in other gifted areas. Plainly, you will be using the status of entrepreneurship in one area of passion so that you can be free to enjoy other areas of passion.

If you are a professional singer and you feel as if it is a calling, you can experience the height of your potential as an entrepreneur. You can travel and be a blessing to others at your heart's desire because your primary business can function without you. When you have a job, you are unable to move freely like this because you will experience a cut in wages or you will be fired. Your loyalty is not to yourself but to your job. The same as self-employment; you will experience financial loss from your customers because you are unable to offer your services, or worse, lose that customer.

You can have a high-paying job that affords you a great lifestyle, but no matter how much money you make at your job, if the days that you show up to your job are not spent doing the things that you are passionate about and truly make you happy, you are just a highly paid slave. It's no different from being a house slave, where you reap more benefits than those picking cotton; the fact is that you are still a slave. Others own you and you have to suck up to them or hear the words, "You're fired".

There are places we need to go but we are unable to go because of a job; there are things we need to do but we are unable to do because of a job; there are gifts that need to be released but are unable to be released because of a job; there are things we need to be but we are unable to be because of a job; there are things we need to accomplish but we are unable to accomplish because of a job; there are books that need to be written but unable to be written. So many potentials are trapped within the cage of a job. In order to experience the joy of freedom, one must rise above the job mentality.

> *You could never lack wealth when you have the freedom to do what you were born to do. Sherique Dill.*

CHAPTER 6

Job Vs Work

There is a difference between a job and work. A person who has not been exposed to their life's purpose sees both as synonymous (identical), but they are not. The truth must be told so that work can be truly appreciated. Your work has nothing to do with the place where you labour. Your work was destined for you before your existence. Your work is a unique solution to a unique problem that exists on earth. Therefore, fulfilling your work makes you a problem solver. Societies of today have craftily connected the concept of job to work. When you think of a job, connect it to skills and labour; when you think of work, connect it to using gifts to complete your life's purpose.

There is one question that you should ask yourself to determine the difference between a job and work. The question is, "Would you stay at your job and labour if you were not being paid?" If your answer is yes, then it marks an area that you have deep passion for and you love so much that the money doesn't matter because it fulfils you. It doesn't feel like a day job. When you truly value something, it is worth more than the money it could put in your wallet.

Reality is that most persons would not stay at their jobs if they were not being paid; this signifies labour, not work.

How I evaluate my job and my work

When I inspire and educate others through writing, I feel divinely high. This is why I'm convinced that this is my area of work; it's my most potent method of Godly influence to planet Earth. My work gives me a sense of peace. I value my work. I would invest my last dollar into it. I'm always curious for new information that relates to my work to ensure that it is of high quality. It fulfils me. When I'm working, my self-esteem is highly boosted; I feel really good about myself to see the things that I could do; to see my potency in high levels. I feel like I'm on cloud nine when I'm engaged in my work. I'm like a drug addict; I'm addicted to true work.

Little is more rewarding than seeing a product that was created by you; it is a beautiful feeling. One of my most memorable moments was when I held in my hand, for the first time, my first published book, "Created to Stand out Not Fit in." I was overwhelmed with joy and happiness. It feels really good to be able to produce something. This was my unique product. So often we seek to use the products of others to obtain wealth when we have our own special product on the inside of us waiting to be unleashed. Using your unique gift as a product means that your product will always be in stock. You won't have to pay those outrageous prices to organizations for their goods and then sell the product for high just to make a profit from consumers. Use your God-given abilities. What are you producing?

When I'm at my job, I don't feel this way. I feel like I'm working far beneath my potential.

Although appreciative for my job, I feel ordinary when I'm there. I have to consistently motivate myself to make it through the day. When I am working (area of potency) I don't need any extra boost; my passion fuels me. When I have to separate myself from my true work because of my job, I get withdrawal symptoms; I'm no longer on cloud nine, I'm more like on cloud one. When I'm at my job, I have no other way of making money; I have to wait until the end of the month for an income refill. When I'm working, I can spontaneously make money. When my income is depleted, I have the ability to sell books at my leisure! If you become engaged in your work, money will flow continuously.

My job is a routine or recurrent experience. When I am working, I can expect the unexpected. It is a platform for me to display my God-given abilities with the world. I get to discover new things about myself. In addition, I get to meet great and successful people. When you discover greatness, greatness you shall attract.

Now, you might ask, "Why are you still there if you feel this way? Why don't you just leave?" Well, wisdom is the principal thing. Leaving a cage before being prepared to will introduce you to more pain than when you were actually in the cage. Why? You know what to expect in the cage. When you come out of the cage, unprepared, you will experience great devastations. It is not an excuse; it's just reality. Therefore, the key is to be prepared by having a well-detailed plan and being in the position wholly to execute this plan with needed resources.

What is a job?

The term *job* relates to corporate environments. Corporate environments hire individuals to labour by using their skills, to perform a group of related tasks, duties, or responsibilities in exchange for wages or payments.

Skills play a major role in jobs

Employers hire employees based on skills or the ability to be taught skills. A skill is a learned ability to complete a task or duty with prearranged results. So basically, you know exactly the result of the skill before you perform it. Skills are normally obtained through institutions, but you can also gain it from experience or self-practice. There are many skills that are manmade because they were created specifically for the corporate world. There are also some natural skills. There are skills such as cognitive skills (ideas), technical skills (things), interpersonal skills (people), time management skills, team work skills, self-motivation skills, etc. If you intend to stay within the job market, then you need a broad group of skills in order to contribute effectively to your organization.

The world is changing rapidly, and you can get burned out trying to keep up with it. Many different types of businesses exist, so your skills would be determined by the uniqueness of your job, whereas with work, everything you need is built into your character.

Anyone can learn a skill through time and dedication. Skills do not set you apart from others because other people can learn the same skills that you learnt; educational institutions are open to all. In other words, you can be replaced; your skills won't qualify you to be irreplaceable.

No matter how hard you try, there are some people in your life that are so good at what they do that trying to replace them will be inconvenient.

Your job can become boring

It is highly possible for you to become bored at your job because you already know the result of your skills. If you're repeating the same duties over and over, how is this conducive for growth?

You may have the ability to perform designated tasks exceptionally well, but that does not mean it is your area of calling, or area of potency. It's just that people have become so desperate for a job that they will learn and like what they have to in order to survive.

Jobs don't really require commitment

When you have a job, you don't have to be committed to it. You can have a new job every year if you choose to. This is the reason why many people don't master any particular thing on a job.

When you are moving from job to job, taking on different types of tasks and duties, your chance of becoming a specialist is compromised. Nothing is wrong with diversity in terms of skills. If you are comfortable just being a Jack of all trades, then learning a multiple range of things would be satisfying for you. However, becoming a master is supreme.

Some people remain on a job for a very long time because they are afraid to leave their comfort zone.

If you were burdened at your job with tasks, would you feel happy taking it home to complete? Your answer to this question will show your level of commitment and dedication. Most people would tell you that they don't love their jobs that much. Performing their tasks is so dreadful that they're excited for knocking off time; they are clock watchers or time keepers. The reason why people will not carry tasks home is because they feel as if it eats up their recreational and family time, and furthermore, they are not energized by it. Work is the opposite; your recreational life is tied up in your work, and it doesn't separate you from your family (spouse, children), because they are free to become involved. This will be discussed more in Chapter 13.

Concept of true work

Unlike a job, to work means to trade your gifts in exchange for fulfilment, happiness, joy, true wealth and true success. Your work is God-given abilities that are pre-determined for problems that exist on earth. In other words, you were deliberately created for a specific problem and the result is pre-determined if you follow your divine purpose.

Here is an example of work according to the Scriptures:

"Now no shrub had yet appeared on the earth[a] and no plant had yet sprung up, for the LORD God had not sent rain on the earth and there was no one to work the ground, [6] but streams[b] came up from the earth and watered the whole surface of the ground. Then the LORD God formed a man from the dust of the ground and breathed into his nostrils the breath of life, and the man became a living being" .Gen 2:5-7(NIV)

Further, it goes on to say, "The LORD God took the man
and put him in the Garden of Eden to work it and take
care of it."

These scriptures show that before the creation of Adam,
The Most High had a specific plan for his life. The Garden of
Eden was in existence before Adam. According to the
scripture, there was work to do before Adam existed. Adam
existed to work. Adam actually enjoyed working. Adam
didn't need training to do his work, which was maintaining
the garden. Adam knew exactly how to perform his work
because it was the reason for his existence.

Misconception of Work being a curse

There is a misconception of work being a curse. There
was a period in my life when I also saw work as a curse
because I was confused about the concept of work. I (as well
as many others) often contemplated as what life would have
been like if I did not have to work and I didn't have to eat
bread by the sweat of my eyebrow.

After being exposed to the concept of true work, it's hard
to pull myself away from it. I have discovered that true work
is more than surviving financially or eating by the sweat of
my eyebrow. Working is a blessing to those who have
discovered the true essence of it. When your number-one
reward for working is to survive financially, you will label
work as a curse because chasing after money takes a lot of
effort. However, when work fulfills you to the point that you
will work without the care of receiving money (because you
are so much in love with it) you won't see work as a curse
because you will not become exhausted; you have fire and

you are full of energy because when you are truly working you perform effortlessly. Work would only be a curse to you if you are not in alignment with your purpose. It is a beautiful and wonderful thing if done within the right environment. The Garden of Eden did not exist for Adam. Adam existed for the Garden of Eden. The same thing with you; your work should not be created for you by others. Jobs are manmade; work was created by The Most High. It is your responsibility to discover your Garden of Eden so that you and your generation can experience the blessings and benefits of true work.

Your financial status has nothing to do with true work (purpose)

If I were a multi-millionaire, I would not be able to stay home and do nothing. Only lazy and slothful people hate to work; they love idleness. Your work does not end when you become wealthy; your work ends when you expire. Your financial status has nothing to do with you completing your due diligence to humanity. You can obtain all the wealth in this world and still be poor because you subtracted purpose from your equation.

When you have found your work, your perception of life will be extremely different. You will have a new appreciation for your life and others.

Work requires no retirement

To retire means to depart, step down, withdraw, stop working or give up work. To withdraw or give up your true work is to be useless. Retirement is not mandatory when it comes to your true work. Work is your lifeline of satisfaction; this is what gives your life meaning, and unlike a job, you cannot just depart from it. If you try to give up your work, you will find yourself right back at it, due to withdrawal symptoms. Retirement is a term made popular in the corporate world, and it normally goes with age. You are required to retire at a certain age even if you're not ready too. This is why some people that retire at the mandatory age don't live long after they retire. They develop and attachment to their jobs, and because they go home to do nothing, they feel as if they don't have anything else to live for. These are the job slaves. They are confused, and their self-worth, self-esteem and value are tied to their job rather than their work. So when they are no longer there, they feel lifeless.

Today, retirement is not only a status of the older generation. There are some people that have retired from their jobs at a young age to explore business opportunities. This is great.

Job slaves work hard because they didn't prepare for their golden years. They are stressed out about how they will pay their mortgage or how they will survive after 40 years of labouring because they didn't manage their income.

Retirement Fund

A retirement fund is money put aside or saved for when you retire from your job. It is often referred to as a pension. Some people die without even seeing the benefits of their job (retirement fund). As a matter of fact, some employees are not afforded this benefit. People are fired or laid off and receive nothing after many years of labouring for organizations. All of your time can be foolishly wasted.

These are the risks of being on a job. This is why when you have a job you must have money management skills. There is something called a personal pension fund, where you (the employee) invest towards your retirement. Most employees are too dependent; they put too much faith in their employer and act irresponsibly. You should not solely rely on pension from the state or contributory pensionable schemes. It is your future; if you are going to labour for someone for 40 years (or whatever long period), make sure that you are investing towards your latter days. This is more important for job slaves because they embrace retirement as the end of working, so definitely they would need saved-up funds to carry them through the remainder of life. People who believe that work is constant can enjoy life to the very end because they don't have to stress about having sufficient funds. Their money flows continuously because it is replenished by true work and intelligent investments.

You cannot quit your true work

Work is not something that you can turn off and on like a switch. You cannot quit your work like how you can quit your job because passion will not allow it. Unlike a job, you will become loyal to your work; you will be committed to it and you will guard it with your life. You will be deeply convicted about it and you will not be able to pull yourself away from it. Your work will become the centre of your life. You will be happy to wake up in the morning, looking forward to what the next day has to offer.

Even if you have a full-time job, you will find some avenue to fit your work within your schedule. This is okay, but don't be surprised if your heart begins to search for a change. When you experience exposure to your work, being at a job will become burdensome because your work will outshine your job. Secondly, your work fills you up so much until you overflow; you will not have enough time to waste. Your work will attract new goals, visions, ideas, and inspirations into your life. You will soon see that job that you never loved for what it truly is: a cage.

You don't go on vacation from your work

One of the best benefits of having a job is vacation. Most people that go on vacation from their job want to be free from it until they return. You don't go on vacation from your true work because it is within you and it keeps drawing you in; it's like a magnet. Furthermore, you love it; you don't want to leave it alone. There is nothing else in the world you'd rather do than to engage in something that you were created to do. I look forward to taking vacations at my job. Why? Duties and assignments become exhausting, so rejuvenation is needed. However, I couldn't take vacation from my work. While on vacation from my job, I find myself occupied with my true work. Work is addicting!

No one can fire you from your true work

The most dreadful thing when you're employed is the thought of being fired or let go. When you control your own destiny, no one can cripple you by taking away your income when they choose to. Many employees live day after day in fear of losing their jobs. It is so refreshing to wake up everyday without the fear of losing your job because you are your own master.

You live on through your works

It is important for you to comprehend that we don't die—we physically expire. When you expire from this earth, you have the ability to exist through your children and through your works. Your energy still exists. One example of this is that as a parent, your children will expose what you have taught them. So when you expire, a part of you continues to remain on the earth. Your philosophies, your standards, principles, and concepts will continue to have influence and be passed down through generations. My beliefs, standards, values and principles were taught to me by my parents, who were taught the same beliefs from their parents, and it goes back generations. The same beliefs, standards, values and principles that I learned are passed on to my children; this is how energy is transferred. You're a form of energy. Energy never dies, and it can never be destroyed. If you can master transferring positive energy, your future generations will be a force to reckon with on this planet and they will live in success. This is one of the ways that you have life after death.

You are not in your area of potency if you aren't able to influence change in people's lives. You should be unforgettable because of this divine influence. So much so, that you can live on in the hearts of people. All mortal bodies have an expiration date. There is no expiration date for immortality. Your spirit is immortal. Your physical body is only a vehicle for your divine spirit, and when your spirit is released from your body, it becomes eternal. Plainly, you are an earthly magnificent god/goddess limited only to the physical body.

It is so important to discover your work because it is your family legacy. It is often referred to as a personal legacy, but nothing is personal when you have a family, so I prefer to replace *personal* with *family*. Personal legacies are responsible for the chaos we see in the world today; people make decisions without considering their family. This is the utmost level of selfishness. Every decision and action will affect your bloodline, and this is why as parents we have to be careful of our actions because our children will reap our harvest, whether it is bitter or sweet.

Having a good family legacy will illustrate how your family, friends and the world remember you.

My beloved grandfather, the late Shervin Simms, loved to say, "May the works I have done speak for me."

I don't want to only read about other people's accomplishments and how they have influenced others or the world; I want people to testify of my impacts as well. Many people don't believe that this is possible for them; they don't feel that they are that great to influence their friends, families, and communities—much less the world. This is due to unbelief and negative thinking. However, if you don't believe, I'm here to tell you that you are great; discover greatness, unleash it and maximize it.

What a disaster it is to born, live, expire, and after expiration there is nothing positively tangible to show that you even existed; you left no legacy on earth for your children to carry on and be proud of. It is sad to expire and not be missed or remembered.

A legacy led by example

The legacy you should seek to leave is a legacy that depicts how you led by example. Create a legacy that reflects good values, morals, principles, true faith and high standards. You should leave a legacy that depicts you as a person who loved doing the right thing and didn't compromise or follow the crowd. What is the right thing? It is actions guided by the laws and principles of The Most High. Leave a legacy that shows that you were guided by a higher power—a power greater than yourself. These things influence people the most.

The following are excerpts from the "Twelve Pillars" by Jim Rohn & Chris Widener:

> *"Live a life that will help others spiritually, intellectually, physically, financially, and relationally. Live a life that serves as an example of what an exceptional life can look like".*
>
> *Let others lead small lives, but not you. Let others argue over small things, but not you. Let others cry over small hurts, but not you. Let others leave their future in someone else's hands, but not you.*
>
> *Leaving a legacy is like planting a tree. As that seed grows into a tree, it will provide seeds, so that future generations can then plant their own."*
>
> *Family legacy surpasses personal legacy! Sherique Dill*

You can pass on true work

When you expire, your work can be passed on so that it can be kept alive. This is the reason for your existence: to transfer what you have been exposed to while on planet earth to the next generation. When you expire, the world will not look up to your children because you had a great job and you made a lot of money. The world will honour and respect your lineage because of your character and your deeds; this holds value, not the status of a job. Once you train your family properly, they will be fully capable of executing your work. This evidence is visible in most generational businesses. When parents expire, often, their children take over the business and keep the vision alive.

It is important to comprehend that your work is not only yours; it belongs to your lineage, and when you don't discover it, you rob them. Chapter 13 discusses the importance of building a family empire. As long as your children are trained to have the business mind-set by growing up in an entrepreneurial environment, they will not become slaves to jobs and they will appreciate what you have left them. Too often, untrained children sabotage their parents' inheritance because of the lack of passion, appreciation and value for what they inherited.

When your family sees the fire and passion for your work, they will pick up that same fire and share the same interests. This is the amazing thing about having ownership. It is also the greatest disadvantage of a job.

If you retire from your organization or you expire, you cannot transfer that job position to your family.

Jobs don't belong to you; you don't own it, so they are non-transferable. When you expire, your son or daughter will not be able to automatically get a job at your organization. They have to qualify if they wish to labour there, just like everybody else.

You own your work; it is your trademark, all rights belong to you and your lineage.

Your children will always remember you when others might forget you. People get so caught up with their personal legacy that they forget the most important thing: family. The most important thing in life is to protect your lineage/bloodline, so don't get overwhelmed helping others at the expense of your own family. Many great leaders put all their efforts towards the betterment of society, and when they die, society forgets them.

When you are a parent, you have the ability to mould your child, teach them your ways, set standards, teach values, etc., which means that they are what you teach them. They're in your image and likeness. Being a good parent is the greatest service that you can give to humanity.

CHAPTER 7

Job Security

One of my greatest inspirations for the title of this chapter came about through my challenge with the fear of failure. I was afraid to step out of my cage because I was in love with security. This was a major setback for me. I saw job security as my friend. Eventually, I became awakened. I see job security now in reverse. Instead of believing that it is my friend, it is an enemy. It was responsible for my mediocrity. Being in a dependent state is dangerous to true success because your highest potential will only be recognized when you accept responsibility for your life. Job security is a stronghold. It will cause you to have unreleased potential and will cause you and your generation to have financial setbacks.

Picture a lion trapped in a cage at the zoo. This lion was placed inside of a cage from the moment it was born. Therefore, the lion doesn't know what roaming the jungle feels like. The lion is not aware of the benefits of freedom or independence. The lion feels safe and secure because there is no need to go out and fight to survive. There are no worries and the lion is certain that his needs will be taken care of.

This lion will become lazy and have less courage and little to no accomplishments, as oppose to a lion that is in its natural environment.

The lion has great expectancy in the zookeeper because if the zookeeper doesn't bring the food and water, the lion will die. The lion has no desire to leave this cage because all of his necessities are being provided. He is now a trained animal, and every action depicts what he has been taught by the zookeeper. Hence, the lion see the zookeeper as his best friend as opposed to its enemy. If the zookeeper were a true friend of the lion, he would remove the lion from his cage.

The zookeeper is very crafty because he knows that if he can gain the trust of the lion by providing for it, he can forever control the lion. So the zookeeper faithfully brings the food, water and necessities. The lion trusts the zookeeper because the zookeeper sustains him, although the zookeeper is responsible for keeping him in captivity. He has no responsibility but to just live. Instead of hunting for his food and ruling the jungle, the lion becomes comfortable with the idea of waiting for someone to bring food, water and everything necessary to his cage for his survival. He is removed from the cage to move about at the discretion of the zookeeper. He has no control over his life or destiny. If the lion remains inside of this cage, he will never know what it means to be the king of the jungle.

Connect this scenario to a job. It's no different. The zookeeper is your employer and you are the trapped king or queen of the jungle. Instead of you being in a physical cage, you are in a cage called a job, which is invisible, and many have been trained to reside within this cage from tender ages, just like this lion. If we were taught how to be entrepreneurs from an early age, we wouldn't chase jobs.

This is one of the main reasons why there is an attachment to security. People are afraid of responsibility. They are afraid to hunt. People would rather live inside a cage and have someone else provide for them in order to experience an easier life. People are afraid to trust themselves; they are afraid to rely on their inner abilities. They would rather trust and rely on the abilities of others because society deposited into their mind that they aren't good enough—that they can only be somebody if they get a good job. Going back to the scenario of the lion, most lions that are kept in zoos are torn apart from their families and lonely, the same way you are apart from your family at a job, unless you work in a family business. Lions that live in their natural environment have what you call a pride; it is a kingdom and unity is their greatest strength. Like lions in their natural environment, we must take control of our family and build our kingdom on this earth.

Many people fear the unknown, which I like to call 'the possibilities' and so they prefer to be certain or assured of things that they believe they can control. Jobs are a form of insurance; people become employees to manage financial risk. This is why when you are in their presence and you talk about becoming an entrepreneur, they try to discourage you. You will hear them say things like, "You're going to leave your secure job to open up a business? That's not a good decision; that's so risky." You should avoid these people; they will talk you right out of your deserved happiness. Everyone is not going to comprehend how jobs are cages; to them, jobs are saviors, and so when you're on your journey of change, you must be aware of whom you share information with.

Money answers all things. You can do nothing on planet earth without money. Does it make sense to depend on another person to give you something that you can't do without? All of humanity has a desire for more money; what makes you think that they would have your best interest at heart? Why would they treat you fairly when it comes to money, something that you can never have too much of because more money equals more power. Since money can be transferred into wealth and wealth can be transferred through generations, it would be wiser to have control of it. Your best bet is to bet on yourself.

Secure: risk free

Some people feel so secure and assured of their job, they have so much trust and certainty in it, that when reality happens (loss of job, fired etc.) they don't know how to manage these changes and they become deeply depressed. The reality is that no matter how secure things may seem to be, nothing is certain; life itself is not sure. To be secure means to be safe from harm, loss or attack—to be free from fears or worry, or you can say secure means to be in a firm position: risk free. People believe that because they have jobs that they are risk free, but that is so far from the truth. Furthermore, the wealthy live by a principle that says, "The greater the risk, the greater the reward." So while you are running away from risk, the wealthy people run to it, and that's why they dominate. It's a brainwashing of society; the things that you have been trained to perceive as risky are not, and the things that you perceive not risky are.

Employment is risky

You may believe that if you have a job it is the safest and most secure way to support you and your family. While you believe that you can depend on the consistency of a cheque, you will live life restricted by it.

Having a job is risky because an employer can turn off all your income just by saying two words: "You're fired." Then you're left with the stress and worry of how you will support your family and pay your bills. This is possible; corporations make decisions based on what's best for them, not you. No one can ever fire you from your work. When you are walking in purpose, you have the opportunity to make daily bread. Some days the reality could be that you might not make a dollar; however, the success of another day can override that loss. With a job, your salary only fluctuates if you receive daily, weekly, or monthly bonuses at the discretion of your employer.

People are no longer living pay check to pay check. It has become worse or unthinkable. Some pay checks are so insufficient that the pay checks are not even lasting until the next one arrives; people are running out of money. I comprehend why salary is called *Gross pay* and why after you have paid all of your expenses it is called *Net pay*. The salary is so minimal that it is gross, and then after you pay all your expenses, you are in a financial net. People who make a decent salary still find themselves struggling to make ends meet at the end of the month, and it's not that they are overspending. Some incomes are so insufficient that people have to decide which bills they are going to pay when they are due. How will you ever rise to financial independence or liberation under these circumstances? When you cut back on all that you could and you are still unable to make ends meet with your salary, this is risky. Being unable to afford an emergency fund because of an insufficient salary is risky. Some of you have goals that you want to accomplish that require a certain amount of money, but you are unable to because the funds are not available to do extra things. These signs indicate an income crisis, which is risky. Employees are sophisticated or professional gamblers.

College Debt

One reason why people run to the safety net of job security instead of aiming for their true work is because as soon as they graduate from college, they are in deep debt. To pay off these debts, they need an income. These debts, believe it or not, are the culprit for many not having the chance to experience financial freedom and independence.

Instead of chasing after wealth, people chase after debts- Sherique Dill

Degrees are becoming more expensive but less valuable because they are very popular; therefore, the market is much more competitive. This then causes the salary for a degree to be less now than it would have been when it wasn't popular. There are people in the job market today with a bachelor's degree, qualifying for just a receptionist position. As well, as there are people with master degrees sitting home unable to get hired because they are deemed overqualified. Does this make sense?

Today, getting degrees holds no guarantees. I am not discouraging people from getting degrees because worldly systems do value them and its added education, but the truth must be told. If you desire them, go ahead and achieve your dreams. However, it makes more sense to obtain education that will help you to build a family empire than for the benefit of a job position. It has to be worth more to you than that. Think about it; what is the primary purpose of a degree? Yes, of course, a job. Only a tiny group of people obtain degrees for self-gratification or for the success of their true work. In reality, you don't need a college degree to be your own master. You spend thousands of dollars on your education to build someone else's empire, die broke and pass debts on to your family instead of wealth. Again, I ask, does this make sense?

Mark Zuckerberg, Steve Jobs, Bill Gates, Sean Combs, Oprah Winfrey and many other wealthy people can attest to this: their entrepreneurial mind-set made them wealthy, not degrees. Who has ever reached the status of true wealth on the premise of college degrees?

Creative intelligence

What truly matters is being able to follow your life's purpose, your ability to be creative with your potencies (gifts) and your ability to execute visions and ideas. There are two types of education: education set by the standards of the world and divine education (education of self, i.e., true education). You are not truly educated just because you have a paper from an institution. True education is displayed when you are in tune with yourself and the will of The Most High; you have focus and clarity in regards to your life's purpose. True education is having the ability to solve a problem that exists on earth. It has nothing to do with curriculum and syllabus; it has to do with mastering your God-given abilities.

People don't value creative intelligence; too often, the worth of intelligence is determined by curriculum and syllabus. People continually get deceived into believing that the only way to learn is through institutions; they often misinterpret education and knowledge. They are not one in the same. Education is information learnt in schools and institutions; it is one method of obtaining knowledge. This is important for people to comprehend because people are driving themselves further into debt because of this false perception.

People who can't afford to go to college are despised, and those individuals are left with a low self-esteem. These individuals will now bring chaos into society because of this false perception that sends out a message that they are ignorant because they didn't obtain education from tertiary institutions. There are some fields that you need extensive training in, such as medicine, law, engineering, etc. However, the truth is that visions create wealth and you don't need a degree to have a vision. The knowledge that you can obtain from experiences (yours or others'), can by far exceed what you can learn in a classroom. Education from colleges is designed and limited, but unlimited knowledge (experiences, self-observation, reading, listening, wisdom from others, etc.) is wealthy, it reaches deep and nourishes your natural abilities and creativity.

The greatest university in the world is a university of books! (Unknown Author)

Borrowing and interests

Borrowing has an oppressive partner: interest. Borrowing and interests will keep you in poverty for a long time if you don't know how to manage your finances. As a matter of fact, interest is worse than borrowing. It is not bad to pay back what you actually borrowed, but when you have to pay interest plus what you borrowed, it will drive you into a never-ending hole. This is why people find themselves having to cling onto their jobs, because in order to meet all of these stipulations, they have to push themselves to the limit of death to make these payments. Some people need two to three jobs to live comfortably. As I said before, these are ways to control people in a modern way. This is why people can only dream of having their own business, because thoughts of their debts are overpowering and they find themselves worrying about money. Having a business can consist of greater borrowing and greater interest, but the potential return will be worth it. Furthermore, when you borrow, it should be for things that have the ability to bring you greater return. You shouldn't put yourself in debt for things that have no ability to bring you rewards: things such as cars, cell phones, jewellery, furniture, electronics, lavish vacations, etc.

Another oppressive financial method that destroys many is credit card debt; people are spending money that does not belong to them, plus interest. Credit cards add to your debt tremendously when you have no spending control, and they prevent you from building wealth. I know that it feels good to spend other people's money, but it will not work out in your best interest. If you feel the need to have a credit card, you should only use them for emergency purposes or things of importance because the interest you have to pay back could keep you in a hole, especially if you aren't making payments on time.

The tactic of borrowing and interest along with other things will keep those who depend on salary subjugated. This is why you have to learn the hidden knowledge; you must learn what to do with money. It's not hidden knowledge because you can't access it; there's no secret to success. It's hidden knowledge because you have to discover it for yourself. You don't get valuable information spontaneously. Why would your oppressors be interested in revealing to you the truth, when their priority is to continuously oppress you? That is why this book exists: to reveal truth.

Economic slavery

During the slavery era, slave masters had to house their slaves, feed them, provide medical care, take care of their families, provide clothes, etc. They were fully responsible for their slaves. When slavery was abolished, was it done in the best interest of the slaves? Craftily, slaves were physically freed, but they were enslaved in other ways, one being through the economy. Economic slavery is much worse than physical slavery. It requires you to feed and house yourself, provide all the necessities of life for yourself and your family but prevents you from acquiring the wealth that you need to live in abundance. Plainly, it is intended to keep you at a limit, to make sure you never rise to a level where you have power. In actuality, it does the same thing that physical slavery does; at the end of the day, you are still powerless.

Poverty is a result of one's mentality. However, economic slavery is very powerful. Not all persons live in lack because they want to or because they are not trying. They are victims of this very ingenious fraud created by governments and organizations invisibly, to continually manipulate. You can never be free if you are a slave to your economy because those who rule the economy rule indeed. The only way to take control of the economy is to create businesses. Jobs make you a slave to the economy, which is why rich people are not hired; they hire people because they comprehend the setup of these systems; they created them. Rich people hardly care about going to college; they search for great ideas and inventions and then hire you, the educated one, to execute their ideas, thus making them rich while you receive wages. This is economic warfare.

Parents often drill the word job into their kids

Parents would be the culprits of advising their kids to "Go to school, get a good education so that you can get a good secure job." I am sure that you have heard this advice at some point in your life from your parents or words of perceived wisdom from the experts. This advice is sound and very appealing, but they are reintroducing millions of people to a lifetime of slavery.

I watch my children fervently for the revealing of their gifts. I don't want to pass a slave mentality onto them. I'm working towards building a family business so that they can carry on my work, not send them to college to build another person's wealth. This is a mentality of a slave. If they go to college, they go to come back and enrich the family business.

I often hear the quote "God bless the child that has his/her own." This is the thought of a slave. As I said earlier, parents should not want to see their children suffer and struggle through life. The reason for ancestors is to pave the way for those who come behind, to make life easier. My desire is to see my children live in freedom and not trapped in the cage of a job, and this should be the desire of all parents: not to teach their kids about job security but to teach them how to build a family empire. So from now on, think, "God bless the family that has their own."

Government Job Syndrome

It is no secret; people know that if they are looking for security, government jobs are most favourable. The stability in government jobs is unmatched. As long as a country exists, governments will exist. Governments will never go out of business because they are crafty when it comes to taking advantage of the citizens; governments will be rich as the citizens stay poor. Therefore, it is no doubt that governments will always have staff, but it is a well-known fact that in many instances government jobs have a low salary. How can the organization that is all-powerful, with the ability to create policies and laws to rule a whole country, not afford to pay their staff well? They have the ability to waste money on things that will not positively affect its citizens but when it comes to giving them a better quality of life, there is no money. Nonetheless, even though people know that these jobs pay little and offer little opportunity for advancement, it does not come close to the best benefit: **security**.

If you would experience termination from a government job, you have to be in extreme breach. In addition, politics play a very important role when it comes to government jobs, and this is why government leaders cope with unproductive and corrupt employees. Their objective is to secure votes.

There are people employed in the government that are not qualified to be there but because of their affiliation and allegiance to political parties they get the jobs.   Hence, the qualified people who are there to make a difference have to deal with people who have the mentality of just wanting a job (security), so chaos starts.   The public has to now deal with people who have no love and passion for what they do, hence the spirit of bad customer service and fruitlessness. Instead of terminating employees who are corrupt and practice poor behaviour on their jobs, they are transferred and permitted to carry on with slackness.   How are you growing as an organization if you choose to transfer problems rather than eradicate them?

Good credit

Another reason why people love secure jobs is that when you have a secure job, you will have no problem getting loans if your salary can accommodate it. Financial institutions will not consider you as a high risk; they automatically assume that you will have that job for a very long time. Unfortunately, small business owners are frequently denied. There are more small business owners than large business owners.   Small businesses drive the economy, but they are perceived as risky. This is a trick to continue to discourage people from accomplishing financial freedom and financial independence.   Don't be deceived.   This is why it is so important to be in control of banks because banks play a vital role in the economy. Most aspired business owners would list finances as the number one reason why they can't get their business off the ground. If people are not able to receive the funds they need to build their visions and dreams, they will continue to struggle in life. We need to empower ourselves and stop depending on help from organizations that don't want to help us.

Salary deduction

Salary deduction is perceivably a good benefit for employees that have secure jobs, such as government jobs. Salary deductions allow employees to get loans quickly because they assure the banks, furniture stores, appliance stores etc., of their payments while you're employed. This is like signing your rights away to these companies because you have no control; the companies have access to your money before you. Is this a benefit or is this another method of oppression? Salary deduction does more harm to some people than good. It provokes those who are mentally weak to purchase things out of covetousness and not necessity. Therefore, it drives employees further into debt.

You have to get to a point where you see beyond the security of a job. Settling for security will have major consequences for your legacy. You have to use wisdom and see past these tricks and craftiness. Preserve your income and invest it into visions that will help you to rise above the cage of a job. Otherwise, you will die in debt and you will be remembered as another secured slave

CHAPTER 8

Make Your Job Status Temporary

Upon entering the corporate world, you should do so with the mentality that it is a temporary status. Work is permanent—not jobs. Too many people make up their beds at their jobs, which contributes to a lifetime of poverty and unhappiness. You should use the corporate environment temporarily to gather knowledge and funds that will prepare you to build your own empire. If you were to research some of the wealthy people today and in the past, you would see that they started out just like you: on a job. Their mind-set is the only thing that separates them from the job slaves. Their ultimate desire wasn't to receive a salary. They were searching for something bigger, something that would create a lifetime of wealth for them and their future generations. Economic power was their driving force; they never had intentions of just labouring for people.

Specialization

When you go to your temporary job, it is important that you make sure that your job caters to your specialization needs. This is important because knowledge is only power when you direct it toward a specific plan and act on it. General knowledge will make you a Jack of all trades, and master of none. In most of the job markets today, there is a shift in regards to college degrees. Today, employers are zooming in on certification. They comprehend that to be certified in a field means to have extensive knowledge in that field as a specialist. Certification or specialization is also a plus when you're opening a business.

Avoid overcrowding your brain

Even though you are limitless and you can do whatever you set your mind on doing, try to focus on the things that make you happy and give you a good feeling. The computer is a replica of your brain. It makes no sense to continually fill up your brain with information that means nothing to you; one day your brain will run out of memory, like a computer. Focus more on knowledge that is connected to your true work; in doing so you will become a force to reckon with. This is important because there are too many people choosing jobs that have nothing to do with their desires or purpose. Everything that you do should be leading you one step closer to your destiny.

This is why I believe in unity; you will never know all the things there are to know in life. If you attempt to try, you will become overburden and burned out. This happens a lot with individuals with the over the top Jack of all trades mentality;

they don't want to rely on others for help. We were not designed to operate this way. We need each other that is why we have different gifts and abilities. What you should do is create a team. When you have a team, you will have access to the expertise of others. For example, why take on the burden of studying law if you have no real passion for learning law? It makes more sense to just have a lawyer on your team. This will help you to stay focused on your true purpose and goals. Doing too many things will weaken your potency. If you want to display your mastering abilities, this is vital. Trying to overcrowd your brain will lead to health issues and defeat. You must be clear on where you want to go and what you want to be. Distraction is a great enemy. Most people that exist on earth don't reach their highest level of potency because they're too busy competing with one another. They want to learn everything so that they don't need anyone. Wise people comprehend the power of unity. Does this mean that you must learn one thing all your life? No. To live means to have a diverse of knowledge, but you must have that true focus and avoid things that will distract you.

See yourself as an apprentice

Many people have to turn to jobs because they weren't fortunate enough to grow up in a family business. Therefore, jobs were their first training ground. If you truly want to accomplish financial freedom and independence, go into the job market with the mentality that you are not just an employee; you are a student. If you have the desire to own a computer business, the best option is to get a job in a lucrative computer organization. Getting a job there would prepare you to be a great entrepreneur in the computer field. You will always attract to you what you are passionate about. Therefore, opportunities will flow for you like a river, again, the law of attraction. Some great doors will open for you because you're in the right environment and you are passionate about what you're doing.

You will learn the skills that are required for success, and here is the best part, you are getting paid to receive this knowledge. This is the greatest benefit of a job. The knowledge that you are receiving is worth more than the salary because no one can take knowledge away from you. When you go to school or college, you are paying for your knowledge. At a job, people are paying you to learn, and this is why you must take advantage of this opportunity. Job slaves actually see this in reverse. They value salary more than the knowledge, which is why they would pass up jobs they are passionate about if the salary is little. When you have the entrepreneurial mind-set, your number-one priority is knowledge, not a salary.

Job slaves don't value the knowledge they receive at their jobs because they didn't pay for it. This is natural. We are beings that appreciate and value things more when we have to pay for it. We see this in everyday life. The knowledge that you get from a job would be discredited and unappreciated because it was free, which is known as experience. However, if you have a degree or certification from a school, employers will perceive it as more valuable because you paid for it or made sacrifices for it. In my view, experience is far greater than a piece of paper from an institution, because those with the experience still have to train those that have the paper. Learning from the experience of others is more rewarding because when you have a mentor and that mentor has already proven the facts about a thing, they are teaching you based on truth, not curriculum or syllabus.

Think and grow Rich: Edwin C. Barnes

In the book "Think and grow Rich" by Napoleon Hill, Hill talked about Barnes having the thoughts of a king; he thought his way into partnership with Edison. This book describes a man who had remarkable faith, determination and a burning desire. How do you feel about yourself? Do you doubt yourself, thinking that the things you desire are impossible to achieve? Do you feel as if you aren't good enough? You have the ability to create your own destiny? If you feel you are good enough, you are correct. If you feel as if you aren't good enough, you are also correct. The universe will manifest your thoughts.

Barnes' burning desire was to become Edison's partner. It didn't happen overnight; it took time. Barnes didn't accomplish his desire instantly. He started off working in the Edison offices, getting a very nominal wage. Hill stated that Barnes was doing work that was unimportant to Edison, but most important to him, because it gave him an opportunity to display his merchandise where his intended partner could see it. Barnes had no intention of failing; failing was not an option for him, and his desires came through because he believed that it could. In actuality, in Barnes' mind, he already saw himself as a partner of Edison, he just needed his inner thoughts to manifest in the physical realm.

Hill also goes on to say that "He did not say, I will work there for a few months, and if I get no encouragement, I will quit and get a job somewhere else. He did say I will start anywhere. I will do anything that Edison tells me to do, but before I am through, I will be his associate." According to Hill, Barnes did not say, "I will keep my eyes open for another opportunity, in case I fail to get what I want in the Edison organization. He said, there is but one thing in this world that I am determined to have, and that is a business association and stake my entire future on my ability to get what I want; He left no possible way of retreat." This is remarkable. Later, an unexpected opportunity came that would make it possible for Barnes to become a partner with Edison, and he did. This remarkable success story shows how the wealthy think. It shows their mentality. Barnes didn't have the intention of working for Mr. Edison. He came there for partnership; however, he had to take a temporary position to achieve his ultimate goal. He started off at a mediocre position, but he used this temporary opportunity to accomplish his permanent desire. This is how people should see their jobs today; it has to have a purpose. What is the purpose of your job? Are you there just for the income, or are you like Barnes, who used his mediocre job position to accomplish his heart's desire?

Other examples of people who started at a job and became entrepreneurs

Oprah Winfrey

Oprah Winfrey came from humble beginnings. She started out hosting a successful television chat show called, 'People are talking.' Her skills in hosting talk shows were realized and Oprah was later recruited by a Chicago TV station to host her own morning show. Achieving tremendous success from her talk show, Oprah later became the host of her extremely popular show called 'The Oprah' that had about 10 million viewers. Currently, she launched her own TV Network called 'The Oprah Winfrey Network.' Oprah went from being a talk show host employee to being an entrepreneur.

Sean 'Puffy' Combs

Sean 'Puffy' Combs, also known as P. Diddy, went to Howard University, where he majored in business administration. Later, He dropped out to pursue an internship at Uptown Records. Although Sean Combs came in at entry level, it led him to become a talent director. Unsurprisingly, Combs didn't stay at this level; he later rose to the level of a vice president in the company. Sean Combs had a vision, in 1993; he started his own production company called Bad Boys Entertainment, where he has accomplished major success. He has worked with artists such as Biggie Small, Mariah Carey, Baby face, Aretha Franklin and Mary J. Blige just to name a few. Combs has also produced one of the most talented rappers of all times: Biggie Smalls. In, 1997, Bad Boy Ent. made a multimillion dollar deal with Arista Records to manage the label. Talk about a great success story; Combs is currently a multimillionaire. This is a great example of starting as an employee and rising to the level of an entrepreneur.

Henry Ford

Henry Ford left his farm home at the age of 16 to take an apprenticeship as a machinist in Detroit. At this organization, he learned to skillfully operate and service steam engines, and he also studied bookkeeping. In 1888, Ford was married and had to briefly move back to the farm life to support his family. Three years later, he was hired as an engineer for the Edison illuminating company. In 1893, his abilities and creativity earned him a promotion to chief engineer. Ford had a vision. His vision led to him developing a plan for a horseless carriage, and in 1896, he constructed his first model, the Ford Quadricycle. He was able to present his automobile plans to Thomas Edison at an executive meeting he attended. In 1903, Henry Ford established the Ford Motor Company. He became renowned for his revolutionary vision, even though he had less than a sixth grade schooling. Ford was considered to be one of America's leading businessmen and one of the wealthiest. What a success story!

CHAPTER 9

High Cost of Living

Only a small group of people can testify that their job affords them the type of lifestyle that they truly desire. These are the people that are at the top of million/billion dollar corporate pyramids: executive levels. To obtain these privileged positions, your skills have to be outstandingly valuable. In addition, these positions are often reserved for certain ethnic groups (foreigners), cultures, genders, etc. You can be an exceptional employee and still be deemed not qualified for these privileged positions no matter how educated you are.

In the corporate world, the majority of employees come in at entry level positions and never make it to the top of the pyramid so that they can be paid extremely well and live a comfortable life with their families. Most employees receive minimum wage or average wage at their jobs. Even those that are being paid a pretty penny find it hard to put their salary to good use because the cost of living is continually on the rise, and the salary is not continually on the rise. Most people experience a promotion every 6 to 10 years, so by the time your employer raises the pay, it is already eaten up by the high cost of living and you are operating at a deficit. This is oppressive. The only way to be victorious and not be defeated by the high cost of living is to be the master of your income stream; otherwise the high cost of living will keep you running back to jobs.

Cost of living

What does the term *cost of living* mean? Well, simply, it is the cost citizens have to pay to maintain a certain standard of living. So, the cost of living index should be set in the best interest of its citizens. It should enhance your quality of life, not downgrade your quality of life. Obviously, the high cost of living is being used to work against the less fortunate.

Politicians have the power to fix the high cost of living for employees. They can ensure that when the cost of living inflates, salary inflates to avoid further poverty. More importantly, they can create policies and laws that will economically empower their people. They know the salary margins and they know that the less fortunate are suffering, yet they favour the rich people so that they can constantly increase their wealth and use that same wealth to oppress the less fortunate. Politicians need you to stay oppressed; this is how they keep power. They obtain power by their promises. Only less fortunate people (the majority) depend on politicians. They are always hoping, and so politicians use this weakness during campaigning for elections; they promise to make life better, but those promises are not executed.

The high cost of living contributes to employers cutting back on hours and eventually jobs, driving up the unemployment rate grossly. When the cost of living rises, things such as health care costs and health insurance also rise. Unfortunately, the first thing people cut back on when they have a money crisis is a healthy lifestyle. There is a saying, "A belly full is a belly full." Well, it makes no sense filling your belly up with things that will contribute to your sickness and death.

People are unable to afford good quality food, so they have to settle for junk food and toxic food because it is cheaper. So, in their bad eating habits, they eventually get sick and die much sooner. In my view, the cost of living keeps rising so that people can keep dying.

Control what you can

You don't have control over the high cost of gas, high cost of food, high cost of land, high cost of school education, high cost of loans and mortgages, high cost of insurance, high cost of utility bills and so forth, but you do have control over the things that you spend money on unnecessarily. In order to accommodate the expensive necessities of life, you must make wise decisions and not allow yourself to be exploited by corporate systems. The truth is that the cost of living is high for people because they allow themselves to get caught up in the web of debt. Companies are master minds in advertising and marketing. They invest millions or even billions just to get you to spend money by creating fashion trends and brands. Their objective is to programme your subconscious mind to see value in their products. They create this illusion because people pay a lot of money for things that they perceive to be valuable, but in reality it has little value. The corporate systems lure you into compulsive buying. One of their greatest tactics is to use celebrities because these are the people that are idolized, and most of the times their fans would covet what they have. Most of the times, these celebrities don't even own what they promote in commercial ads; it's all about manipulation and wealth for them while you remain poor.

Don't become a victim of compulsive buying through deception. Don't believe that the power is in the hands of the system, when you have the utmost power. People often complain about the high cost of living as if there is nothing that they can do, and so they continue with this lifestyle. These corporate systems prey on the mentally weak and those who aren't clear in regards to their destiny.

Your cost of living doesn't have to fit in with the world's cost of living. You can set your individual standards; don't set your standard based on the world's perception. Your number-one priority is to live a fulfilled life and leave wealth for your children, and this journey will require you to make sacrifices. These products that people consistently chase after lose value every day. It is planned to operate this way. Companies don't want you to have the same product for years. They have to phase it out so that you can keep buying the latest products; this is how billions are made. Can we blame the companies? Certainly not, everyone desires currency and wealth. However, you must be intelligent enough to keep more of what you have than spending it foolishly. If you are passionate about buying, use that same energy to buy stocks. For example, since you love buying phones buy a stock in a phone company—redirect that energy.

Your cost of living will be higher than it needs to be because of the bad decisions that you make. People are putting themselves in debt just to satisfy others. For example, we all would agree that today having a car makes life much easier in regards to movement; however, why purchase a car that you can't afford? People put themselves in huge debt at the bank because of lust, selfishness and greed. If you can't buy a car with cash, then you can't afford the car. In addition, cars depreciate the moment you drive off in it. Cars are not assets; they are liabilities, so why put yourself in extreme debt for others to have a false perception of you? A car becomes an asset if you use it to provide an income for you, such as a taxi or tour bus.

Recreational life

Recreational life is extremely important because it brings balance; life can't always be about working. Success means nothing without family, so having a recreational life creates that environment where you can spend time with your family and have fun.

Unproductive recreational life

People are spending too much money on unproductive entertainment. Control is needed in this area. Some people party too much, and they spend more money on fun than avenues that have the ability to create a higher quality of life. Some individuals are addicted to drugs, liquor and promiscuity instead of being addicted to their life's purpose. Partying and having fun more than productivity is a problem. Too much entertainment is wasted time. If you are an individual that loves the club life, think about how much money this lifestyle is costing you. From buying a nice outfit for each occasion to always being at the bar having drinks and treating others, these little things add up. It is common for humans to be more attracted to negativity than positivity. Most people would rather buy a pair of shoes that they don't need than a book that will empower them. This shows a lack of self control.

Women are highly targeted

A lot of women spend a ridiculous amount of money on beauty and fashion. There is nothing wrong with investing in you and taking care of yourself. This is important; however, a lot of women go overboard with beauty and fashion. They become obsessed with it. Men waste money too, but a nation is only as strong as the women in it. Why? Women have the largest responsibility of nurturing the family and training the children; her concepts will affect generations. In most cases women are around their children more and this is why their role is very vital. Women have the responsibility of being vigilant when it comes to the finances in her family, and so she should not be wasteful. Women are powerful beings. There is a saying that says "Behind every successful man is a good woman." Actually, on the side of every successful man is a good woman, because both are as equally important when it comes to securing the future of the family. You can read Proverbs 31, which talks about the qualities of a virtuous woman. One of the qualities that stood out to me is a woman's ability to invest in businesses. This scripture will show you the pivotal role a woman plays in her family.

It is drastically wrong to spend tons of money on things that have no ability to improve the quality of life for your family. When you have a family, you must become altruistic. This is about the happiness, triumph and economic power of your bloodline. The beauty industry will create this picture to lure you into a fantasy world, where to be beautiful means to spend two to three hundred dollars on a bulk of weave. In addition, to be beautiful according to the world means to have light skin, hence the addiction to skin lightening cream. Some women don't even desire to wear their own nails anymore. Beauty is a multi-billion-dollar industry that feeds off of the weak obsession. It's almost taboo for women to not wear makeup. The face powder, to lipstick, lip liners, eye shadows, mascara, blushes, etc. were all created for you to spend money as a woman. In addition, women have to be careful purchasing these products because many of these name-brand beauty products and cheaper products are toxic and detrimental to their health.

The fashion industry will manipulate women to spend a lot of money on clothes, shoes, bags, etc. These systems deceive women to connect beauty with materialism. To feel beautiful because of fashion and things of vanity is not real or true; it's an illusion. What would possess a woman who is barely surviving financially, or who is just over broke, to continually sacrifice the well-being of her family to meet the beauty standards of the world? Only mental slaves use materialism to boost their self-worth; furthermore, true wealthy people hardly spend money on materialistic things; they are more interested in preserving wealth and transferring wealth to their bloodline; don't be deceived by their pictures and billboards advertisements. This is why most families are in poverty; they are not putting their money to good use. They are too busy getting caught up in the deception of these evil systems. These evil systems are designed to pull every dollar out your pocket, transferring your money to their families, who then use the same money to further oppress you.

This is only the tip of the iceberg in regards to the things women find themselves spending money on—money that should be saved up and invested towards the future of their children.

"Beauty fades, wealth lasts through generations"
Sherique Dill

People must learn how to live below their means, not above it. If you live below your means, you will have funds available for investment. You won't be able to become free financially if you set your standard of living above your means. The challenge is that most employees are so burned out at their day job that even the thought of labouring or doing extra things when they knock off is dreadful. So they put all their eggs in one basket. Also, their salary is so limited that they don't have the surplus to invest in things that will generate residual income or passive income. Investments should be made from your surplus. Most wealthy people invest from their surplus—money that they have saved that they don't need urgently—and they use it to get a potential return. You shouldn't make investments with your life savings or your emergency funds, because investing is a risk; it could be lost and then you're left with nothing. Unfortunately, this is not the case for the majority of people. A lot of people barely have a thousand dollars saved up for emergency in their bank accounts, much less for investments.

If you feel overburdened by the high cost of living, then evaluate yourself. Write everything down that you spend money on (spending tracker); this will help to keep you conscious of spending activities. Also, you must have a budget. You should know all of your expenses and then put money aside to accommodate those expenses. You should set a limit amount every week for daily needs and commit to not going over that limit amount. This takes discipline and only the disciplined will accomplish wealth.

Passive income

Large passive income or residual income is a method that leads to financial freedom. Passive income is an income method that you create once but it continues to generate income. Little work is required to maintain it. However, you must put in the work to get the results that you desire. Setting up a new stream of income takes a lot of hard work, time and dedication. Some examples of passive incomes are rent from property, royalties (music etc.), dividends and interest from owing securities (stocks and bonds), pensions, licensing your idea, continuity programs and franchising. Writing a book is passive income, even though you have to market it, you can sell it over and over again once it's created. Having a salary is non-passive because if you stop labouring, you don't get paid and this is one of the many reasons why it is a cage.

CHAPTER 10

True Success

You feel a great sense of accomplishment because you're at the height of your career and you have status at your job. You have the accolades and the degrees from college. You own a nice car, you live in the house you always wanted, and you're financially comfortable because the salary is great. You have a beautiful family that is sustained by your job, so what more can you ask for? All of the above are great achievements, but is it true success?

What is success?

Success is the accomplishment of an aim or purpose.

What is true success?

There are many ranges of success depending on what you're trying to accomplish. However, true success is the completion of your life's purpose. True success creates a high level of happiness and fulfilment. You will know without a doubt that you are on your course of destiny. Other areas of success are life's bonuses, but they mean nothing if you can't complete the original intent The Most High has for your life. In order to claim true success, you must be a problem solver; you must be able to solve problems that affect humanity. Lives must be changed from your solutions. Plainly, it's your ability to positively influence. You are the only person that knows the truth of your success. People around you might perceive you to be in triumph due to materialism, but they don't know the truth of your success.

You cannot interpret your success as true because you have a nice job, nice car, nice house, a big bank account and all of the things that cater to your flesh. These are the things that most people seek to accomplish. They seek to enjoy the vanities of life and have an abundance of riches, but they never search deeper: deeper into their existence. Even the animals fulfil their reason for existence; how did humanity lose their way?

Do you know why you exist on earth? Most people cannot answer this question. Not being able to pinpoint your reason for existence is a tragedy. This is the main foundation of why people are frustrated and bitter with life; they are not engaged in things that give their life meaning. If you keep engaging in things that mean nothing to you, you will keep attracting things that mean nothing to you.

Problems exist on earth that can only be solved by your creativity and your uniqueness. The earth loses tremendously when you live a life void of purpose. Every solution to a problem comes through the womb of a woman, and this is why life must be treasured. Babies are not just being born; solutions are being born. Plainly, you are not just a human being. In the Creator's eyes, you are a divine solution to earth's problems. The reason why you were sent to earth is greater than you.

Imagine South Africa without Nelson Mandela. Imagine if there was no Marcus Garvey. What if Dr Martin Luther King Jr. decided not to fulfil his purpose? What if Mahatma Ghandi did not fight for a better quality of life for Indians? What if Bob Marley didn't release his music of consciousness? Bob Marley left a great legacy in Jamaica and around the world for his children to be proud of. What if Thomas Edison or Henry Ford neglected their passion? These world changers brought solutions to earth problems.

The reason why people are idle, unsuccessful and hopeless is that they have no focus and clarity when it comes to life; their primary aim is to just live.

When you find your life's purpose and you know exactly where you want to go in life, you will find happiness.

People lose their way because they stray away from The Most High and they don't maintain their relationship. You cannot cut yourself off from your Creator and source of life, expecting to live a fulfilled life; if you do this you will die unsuccessful.

It is important for people to also realize that true success will also not be accomplished through wickedness and wrongdoings. How can you feel successful in a thing if accomplishing it contributed to the pain and suffering of someone else? On your journey to success, you must always do what's right; if not, you will pay for your wicked deeds. What goes around will definitely come back around, a true fact of life.

Why should you want to achieve success by stepping on the backs of your brothers and sisters? This is not true success; it is false success. True success is earned through righteous works.

Earthly treasures, Heavenly treasures

Matthew 6:19-20 says, "Lay not up for yourselves treasures upon earth, where moth and rust doth corrupt, and where thieves break through and steal. But lay up for yourselves treasures in heaven, where neither moth nor rust doth corrupt, and where thieves do not break through nor steal. For where your treasure is, there will your heart be also" (KJV). This clearly shows that true success is beyond the earthly realm.

Earthly treasures are materialistic things: things of vanity. Earthly treasures are those things that fade away or vanish. Heavenly treasures are eternal: righteous deeds. Your deeds are either agreeable (right) or disagreeable (wrong). It is your ability to have a positive influence on the lives of others. Your good deeds or heavenly treasures will benefit you and your bloodline on earth and after you have expired.

If you want to lay up treasures in heaven, you must solve the problems that you were designed to solve.

Success is already inside of you

Greatness belongs to all of us, and it is already inside of us; it is up to each of us to discover our success gene. It's up to us to recognize our divine state.

The Most High is waiting for you to ask for the things you desire, and they will be given to you once you believe. The success gene does not favour any particular person or family. If you are a part of a lineage that has an unsuccessful history, you have the ability to change that. It can begin with you; you can restore your family lineage. Your success gene is only awaiting activation.

You are responsible for your success, and you can't blame others if you aren't getting what you deserve out of life. You don't exist to make a living from a random job, retire, receive a pension, and then expire, fading away to non-existence. You exist to be more than that.

One of a person's greatest enemies is lack of confidence. Lack of confidence exists many times because of past experiences, perceived failures, and constant negative environments. These experiences can cause you to stay within your comfort zone because you feel insecure. You are afraid that you will not get the results that you desire. This is a mental battle.

Don't allow your job status to determine your destiny or affect your self-esteem because what you are doing is only a small portion of what you can do.

If you are afraid to accomplish the things you desire because of past hurts and pain, the time is now to accept what happened and get rid of the fear and negative energies. These circumstances happen to make you stronger and to solve other people's problems.

Affirmations

You must know the power of your subconscious mind and use it to accomplish success. The subconscious mind stores recurrent orders made in faith, whether it is negative or positive. This means that whatever you think, say or do through belief is stored within the subconscious. If you believe that you are not good enough, then you won't be; your subconscious mind will remind you of this everyday. If you believe that you are a failure, then you will always fail; your subconscious mind will carry out this order. Use your subconscious mind to create your reality. You can reverse the negative mentality that has been embedded within your mind from your environments. How can you do this? Well, by re-training the mind; it's a process of transformation. Plainly, it's undoing what has previously been done to you mentally. Make your affirmations every day. You must recognize your weaknesses but focus more on your strengths. Stop focusing on your faults and focus more on the good in you; focus more on what you want out of life. Declare that you are successful. Declare that you are walking in your purpose. Declare that you are a person of determination and persistence and that you are saturated by passion. Declare that you will accomplish your desires. Declare that you will be set free from all cages. If you want to become an entrepreneur, say that you are an entrepreneur; call these things into being and act like you already have it. I'm an inspiring entrepreneur. I have been to many entrepreneur seminars because I want to attract this energy to me. By doing this, I think like an entrepreneur and I meet great connections that are gateways to where I desire to be. Each of us has our unique affirmations; be sure to write them down. Say them every day and be passionate about it. If you don't have the time to read them, record yourself and listen to it as often as you can. The key to re-training or re-transforming your mind is to saturate your mind with positivity so that your mind won't have any vacancy for negativity. The mind is so magnificent that it will act however you tell it to act.

True measurement of success

The measurement of your success should be based on what you have done versus the things that you should and could have done: your potentials. If you still have desires within your heart to do things that it is possible for you to do and you have not done them or you don't plan to do them, then you haven't reached your highest level of true success. No desire should be pending. You might not live long enough to accomplish all the things you truly desire, and this is why generational goals are important. Also, you must explain to your children the purpose and power of a generation.

Too often people seek to compare their life with other people. They look at the success of others and then try to measure their success based on what others have done. This type of behaviour will only lead you to a life of covetousness. Success stories are different and incomparable. Search for your own unique story of success. The only person that can judge your level of true success is you and The Most High because only you and the Most High know the full details of your life's purpose. You are not successful because others perceive you to be; you are successful because you know within your heart that you are in alignment with your life's purpose.

Feeling empty

It is such a catastrophe to accomplish much in life, yet feel empty—to have success in meaningless areas, areas that don't add joy or fulfilment to your life. Many find themselves in these circumstances. There are lawyers, doctors, accountants, bankers, actors, businessmen, etc.: perceivable successful people, trapped in professions that have nothing to do with their purpose in life. Sadly, later in life (sometimes never) they realize that they have no true passion for their profession; they realize that it was not their divine calling; it was someone else' dream, but not theirs. They were forced to live in this dream that later became their nightmare. This is a sad reality. You can only trick yourself for so long, and eventually the sadness and dissatisfactions will begin to affect you. The reality is that after you are done putting on a smiling face, you have to go home and face the fact that you don't love what you do. This is why you shouldn't envy people. Many envy people because of their materialistic success; however, they don't know their story, or if their success is true.

Vision leads to success

When you are connected to your purpose, you will begin to have true visions. You will have clear directions on where you want to go in life, and this vision will bring you success. What you should be seeking is an alignment between The Most High's will and your vision.

If you have a vision that is not written on paper, consider it to be weak; it has no power until you write it down. Writing it is the first physical act of manifestation. You have to be brutally honest with yourself. List all your strengths and all your weaknesses. Then you should write down what you would like to see happen because doing that would make it more believable, you must learn how to pull the vision out of your head and write it on paper. Now this is very important;

share it *only* with people that you trust and people that you have chosen to be a part of your team. Share it with positive people—people who will motivate you to go for it, and you can do whatever you set out to do.

What is a vision?

Desire is birthed from vision, and vision is birthed from your life's purpose. You can't desire things that you haven't yet seen. A vision is a clear picture of your destiny. It is something you see with your mind's eye, and it has nothing to do with your current reality or position. Visions must be clear and lucid because you are depending on them to direct you to the never-ending possibilities of the future.

There are true visions and false visions

False visions create weak desires. They are temporary desires, and most of the times they exist because you saw someone else succeeding in something, so you seek to copy them. False visions are visions that you just run with, having no plans on how to achieve it. False visions have no connection to purpose; therefore, it will not bring about true success. Don't confuse ideas with visions. It is important for you to fully comprehend that anyone can have an idea and execute their idea; ideas come a dime a dozen. Ideas can pop up in your mind at any moment.

Also, don't set your destiny on hand-me-down ideas. If someone has to give you an idea, you will have no real desire for it. Ideas are bonuses; having a vision for your life is key. Why? Your visions existed with you from the moment you were born. Ideas are spontaneous. They can be major distracters because they are falsely perceived as visions. Stay away from journeys that The Most High did not send you on. On your journey of life, always remember that it's either The Most High's way or no way! All roads that are not paved by The Highest of High will lead to chaos and destruction! These journeys are self-made journeys that cause you nothing but pain and heartache, never bringing forth happiness.

The vision for my life keeps me energized. When I feel like giving up, when I feel discouraged and disappointed, and when I feel like condemning myself, I find strength in my vision because it is the ultimate plan that The Most High created for me, and who am I to go against the plans of The Most High.

CHAPTER 11

What's your Plan B

Most people are afraid of failure. This fear is dangerous, and it will hold you back if you don't change your perception of it. The only way that you can truly fail is if you never try or if you quit. If you set out to accomplish your desires and the result leads to defeat, don't be discouraged; the more disappointments and perceived failures the more you will attract success. Defeat is only temporary. The route to success is to fail. This is so because we learn from experiences. When you execute a plan and meet temporary defeat, this temporary defeat will teach you not to go that route again; it will boost your creativity and release unexpected potential. Each failure gives you the opportunity to discover a solution to a problem. Does this mean that you should plan to fail? Certainly not, but if you meet it on your way to success, never let it destroy you. Keep moving forward.

A dangerous type of fear is the fear of criticism. This fear would cause you to procrastinate or withdraw from making decisions, accomplishing goals and releasing your high potential because you fear what people will think.

I had to renew my way of thinking when it comes to fear. It is false evidence appearing real, and most of the times the things that we are afraid of are harmless. You must have the ability to separate fantasy from reality. It all comes down to self-confidence; you must believe in yourself. Fear comes to destroy your faith and confidence. It will take away hope for your aspirations. Failing is the birth of great potentials, and for every failure, you will receive equivalent success. High failures equal high success; low failure equals low success.

It's impossible to go through life void of failures

Failure is inevitable. As long as you have life, you will experience failure. So it makes sense to re-program your mentality to see failure as your friend.

The only way failure will become your friend is if you are prepared to go through pain, heartaches, suffering, setbacks, and discouragements. Obtaining success is not easy; there were many things that people who were successful had to endure: years and years of repeated defeat. Life will throw hurdles at you, so you have to be determined and persistent, but most of all you must have that burning desire for your vision. This burning desire will cause you to ignore all defeats. It will give you a strength you never knew you had because you desire nothing more in the world than to see your plans manifest. Those who have a burning desire will pay no attention to the route of their success; they only care to achieve it.

Regardless of your emotions, you must be loyal to your desires. You must practice great habits, overcome idleness, reject laziness and fear, and also be committed to schedules and goals.

Since you know now that failure is inevitable, you must also know that the only way to overcome it is to have a plan. If you set goals and try to accomplish them without a plan, your defeat will be recurrent, not temporary. The greatest mistake that you could make on your journey to success is to not have a plan. Having a plan would also help you to be conscious of opportunities because they are often unanticipated, and if you are not conscious, you will lose because you will be unable to decipher opportunities from defeats.

No wise person will go through life without a plan, and without guidelines; if you are living this way, it's time to change that. This is why I comprehended that before I leave the cage of a job, I must have a plan and definitely a Plan B. Most employees hardly believe in having a Plan B because they feel no reason to; they feel secured. However, everyone should have a Plan B, especially employees. As I noted earlier in this book, having a job is risky. As an employee, what would you do if you go on your job tomorrow and you hear the words, "You're fired'? In addition, what if the company you labour for is bankrupt and they cannot afford to pay you? What will you do? What plans do you have in place to survive? What will your reaction be? Will you feel devastated because of their decision or will you walk away with a smile because you have a business plan that you always wanted to execute? Will you see this as a crisis or as an opportunity? Will this decision drive you further into poverty or will this decision attract more wealth from the plans that exist? Being fired or let go from your job without a plan means that you have given your employer supreme control over your life; it means that you had too much trust in them, more trust than you had in yourself.

Have a blueprint

It makes no sense executing good anger when it comes to the direction of your life, if you don't have a plan. This will only make matters worse and affect your health. It is depressing to know you are in a bad situation and then helpless because you have no way out. If you want change, you need a plan. If you don't have a plan, you will have no focus and clarity in your life, and you will end up in any direction. You need something to guide you. If you don't plan your life, your life will plan you, or others will plan your life. Plans are the result of desire. If you don't have a plan, it's because you have no desire.

You need to know what your purpose is; then you need to know why you want to leave your cage (job) because these are the things that will give you the will to never go back. When you are about to make decisions, always ask yourself one question: Why? The word *why* signifies the purpose of a thing and will remind you of the reason behind your actions.

What is a Plan B?

Not having multiple plans is the number one reason why people fail. As soon as they meet defeat with their initial plan, they throw in the towel.

Anything that you set out to do that has meaning and has the ability to improve your way of life, and that of your generation, will meet temporary defeat. This temporary defeat represents the value of what you are pursuing. To avoid being overcome by temporary defeat, you must be prepared to draft as many plans as needed to accomplish your goal. When the term Plan B is used, it represents having a secondary plan in case the first plan fails. It is also a contingency plan or a worst-case scenario plan, backup plan, or a disaster-recovery plan. This type of plan is simply a secondary or substitute course of action that needs to exist in the event that the primary approach fails to function as it was planned too.

The Plan B method is very successful—so much so that probably all who have obtained wealth believe in the principle because they know that failure is inevitable and they must find different ways to accomplish their desire. It will allow you to adapt to changing circumstances with confidence and strength, remaining stable and not crippled by a perceived crisis.

Having a Plan B doesn't mean you are doubtful

Now you might ask, "Why should I need a Plan B?" You may say that you are living by faith and that you will make it the first time. The plan that you have seems so well written and looks so perfect, so it could not possibly fail; it has to work. You may feel as if making a Plan B means that you doubt Plan A. This is a critical mistake. Religion today has created a fantasy world for most people, where they believe that blessings will drop from the sky instead of them being strategic and working towards success. In addition, religious people believe that success should come to them the first time, when the facts is clear from those who have accomplished a high level of success. The facts show that previous to success, many plans will fail.

Thomas Edison had a desire to create a lamp that could be operated by electricity. Edison experienced more than ten thousand temporary failures before he became successful. What if he gave in to those failures?

Steve Jobs encountered many temporary failures before he achieved a high level of success. Steve Jobs was a co-founder of one of the most successful computer industries today: Apple. One of his many temporary failures was when executives of his own company phased him out because they no longer believed that he was good for the company and he was holding the company back. Steve Jobs left Apple. I'm certain that at this period in his life he felt a strong sense of failure and disappointment; he had to leave his own company. However, he didn't allow temporary defeat to stop him. He created another business called NeXT, Inc., a hardware and software business, then an animation company, which he called Pixar Animation Studio. This studio went on to produce popular movies such as Toy Story, Finding Nemo and The Incredibles. He later merged with Walt Disney, where he achieved tremendous success, making him the largest Disney shareholder. Apple later bought the company NeXT, and a year later Steve Jobs was hired as CEO of his co-founding beloved vision. He reinvented Apple and became a revolutionist. His visions brought evolution to modern technology, with products such as the iPad, iPod, iPhone, iTunes and the MacBook. Failure surely brought Steve Jobs success.

You are not questioning your faith because you decide to have a Plan B. You will not know what your best route is until you try the route. There is no guarantee that the route you use will take you to your destination. You just have to keep trying until you reach the goal. Like I mentioned earlier, each time a plan fails it gives you more knowledge.

Plans are just routes

Plan A is just a route; it is not the goal. Think about it this way: If you decide to go to a shopping mall, the mall is your goal; it is your destination. Your first plan, Plan A, may include you driving on the main highway to get to your destination. However, when you get on the highway, there is traffic on the highway that is causing major delays. What do you do? Do you give up or feel like you have failed? Do you continue on your primary route and waste time being idle just because you want to remain faithful to Plan A, or do you remember all those little corners that can take you straight to your destination in a different way? It's called finding an alternative route. It could be a bit more inconvenient, involve more pain and heartaches, it could have a few more turns and stops, but in due course, you will make it.

The goal did not change, just the way you got there. People do this in their normal everyday life; they make adjustments all the time, but when it comes to their life's plans they forget these concepts. Nothing in life is guaranteed to work the way you plan for it to work, no matter who you are or how spiritual you may be. Things happen that are unexplainable, but I will guarantee you that if you are persistent, always creating new plans when one fails, you will accomplish your goal. All things will work together for good.

When I wrote "Created to stand out not Fit in," I was schedule to publish and release it in 2014. This was my ultimate goal for 2014. However, I was not able to accomplish my goal at that time due to unexpected obstacles. At first, I was discouraged because things didn't work out the way I planned them too. In addition, it seemed as if my ultimate goal was so far away. I had to regain my strength and confidence and find other ways to bring this goal into manifestation. I had to detour away from Plan A and become adaptable. In June 2015 (Plan B), I was able to print, publish and have a release party for my book. I still accomplished the goal. If I would have tried to make Plan A work, it probably would not have turned out as successful as it did. The Most High will always direct you to the right route. If something doesn't work out the way you planned it to, have no fear, there is a better way.

Here is another example. If you are a person that has the ultimate goal of getting married, there is no certain way to find that person. Plan A may be to meet this person in the church you attend. Plan B may be to meet that person at work. Plan C may be to allow your family or friends to introduce you to someone. Plan D may be to use the privilege of online dating. None of these routes may even work; life may bring you that special person in a way you never even imagined.

Sometimes you might exhaust all the letters in the alphabet trying to get to your destination. What is important is that you accomplish your goal. Do not allow routes to distract you. We get so caught up on routes that the goal is right in the front of our faces and we don't recognize it. Don't be so loyal to one plan that it jeopardizes the goal.

Very few things go the way we plan. When you have challenges with your goal/goals, success is testing how you manage failure before it can trust you. Always remember that although some plans will fail you, you need them; it is a requirement for those who desire true success.

We really think that we are in control of life and that life should always be kind to us. We may look at other people and see them in their glory and triumph, not taking the time out to investigate their troubles and what they had to endure to accomplish a life that is kind and beautiful. Life is not freely kind to anyone; if you want a kind life, you must pay the price. There is a hefty cost for happiness and true success!

CHAPTER 12

Abuse of Leadership

If you have the responsibility of being the head of a group of people, where you are expected to guide and direct, you are a leader. There are false leaders and true leaders. False leaders are abusive; they use their power of influence to oppress. True leaders have a high sense of value for those whom they have the privilege of leading. True leaders are physical guardian angels.

In the corporate world, managers or supervisors are leaders. Some of them have the wrong concept about their role of influence. They belittle or degrade the people whom they have the privilege of leading. They don't comprehend that they should uplift, encourage and empower. They should promote growth and development by training their mentees. They should motivate, inspire and most of all positively influence their mentees for the betterment of the organization and extensively the earth.

In some job environments, employees fear their managers. This is not true leadership. Great managers have a good relationship with the people they manage. Leaders should not lead through fear. Also, many managers allow their personal issues and emotions to get in the way of their professionalism because they have no self-control.

is clear from experience and observation that many of these individuals in the position of leadership are not deserving of it; they do more harm than good. I am certain that most of you that are reading this book have had at least one bad experience with an unqualified leader.

In the words of Coach Marshall Goldsmith, "What got you here won't get you there." In other words, you would need much more than the qualities that awarded you the supervisory post to be a great leader. All of us are leaders in our own special way; you can be a leader of positivity or negativity, but to be a true leader, you must have divine qualities.

There are many true leadership qualities. True leaders must be grounded in righteous beliefs. They must have compassion but still be able to make strong decisions. They must have the ability to make good judgments. True leaders should have a spirit of humility and not arrogance. True leaders must be able to have clear visions and have the ability to execute their visions through others. They must have love and passion for what they are doing—a love and passion that derives from purpose. When you are a leader at your job, you should be able to influence your staff to make positive changes, and this is how you become their inspiration. If you are unable to inspire, you are not a true leader. In addition, true leaders must have the ability to have good communication skills. They must have the ability to inspire trust and display loyalty. True leaders make great sacrifices, and their actions and decisions always benefit the greater good. True leaders have character. In order to be considered a true leader, you must be capable of defending and protecting the people that you lead. You must be on the battlefield of life with them until you're unable to fight anymore; it's not only about being a leader but a true friend.

Corporate leaders

Corporate leaders obtain leadership positions for reasons such as education, salary, experience, physical appearance, favor, seniority, etc. However, none of these things qualifies a person to lead. I comprehend why leadership is described as a gift from The Most High. Taking up courses on leadership doesn't qualify you to be a true leader. Taking up courses can help to develop you better when it comes to leading, but to be a true leader, these important qualities must be embedded within; they must be a part of your character and nature. Many managers or supervisors have no clue how to guide their staff; they have no clue how to develop them and how to accomplish goals through them; furthermore, many of them are self-centered. True leaders care about their team more than themselves: they are altruistic. You cannot be deemed a true leader if your goal is to be recognized and awarded. Why? Well, true leaders comprehend that in order to have a productive and loyal team, the credit must be given collectively, and not take the credit for themselves. As a leader, taking the credit for your team's success will qualify you for defeat and failure. This type of behavior will cause your team to withhold their potential, and they will no longer be efficient and productive.

Leadership positions should be given to people who comprehend teamwork. Also, as a manager or supervisor, you should comprehend that if you are oppressing your staff to the point where they are failing, you are a failure. Your success or failure is in the hands of the people that you lead. This means that the validity of your leadership can be tested by the productivity of your staff.

Difference between self -confidence and arrogance

There is a misinterpretation about self-confidence and arrogance. Some people get confused when it comes to the meaning of self-confidence, so they practice self-depreciation. You should always feel good about yourself and believe in yourself. You should have self-love and self-worth. When you are overbearing with your confidence, always bragging about yourself to the point where you are offending others, and having an overbearing feeling of self-importance where you underestimate others, you can consider that to be arrogance. You should not manipulate people's perception of you to get them to see you as perfect or flawless. Most people who display this type of behaviour seek to divert attention from their imperfections, weaknesses and failings by overrating themselves.

Leaders need to have high self-confidence because they are dealing with people's lives, and if leaders don't believe in themselves, how can they expect others to? Also, if you don't believe in yourself as a leader, you are not qualified to lead because you can't be trusted. Your mentees will not respect your decisions. People respect strength, and if you don't believe in yourself, you are a weak person. When you are confident and you display true leadership, your mentees will admire you; they will be loyal to you and there is nothing that they wouldn't do for you.

Many people exist that don't love themselves and have no confidence, so when they interact with you, they want you to tone down. Their envy causes them to falsely categorize your confidence as arrogance. The people that would confuse your confidence with arrogance crave and envy the confidence that you have. Nothing is wrong with feeling good about yourself or talking highly of your strengths as long as you aren't degrading others. There is a saying that says, "You shouldn't blow your own horn". However, I disagree to an extent because if you are depending on others to blow your horn, the horn wouldn't blow. No one on this planet can tell your story better than you, and no one on this planet can testify of your good works better than you. To depend on people to tell your story alone is a disservice to you. Why wait for others to talk about your good works? Or why wait until it's your funeral for people to get on the stage and give a speech on "As I knew her or him"? Life taught me a great lesson; you have to appreciate yourself and not depend on the appreciation and awards of others; this has nothing to do with arrogance, this has to do with appreciation of self.

When you are exposed to your life's purpose and you realize your potential, you start to see yourself in a different way. You are connected to a higher source; you are in tune with who you are, so you can't help but to speak positivity over your life, despite the request from others to speak down of yourself. This is very crucial for leaders. Continue to love yourself in a humble way despite the unproductive criticism.

Purpose and leadership

You should not have the privilege of leading people if you do not have a sense of purpose. You must know your reason for existence before attempting to lead or influence. If you don't have a sense of purpose or comprehend the reason for your existence, you will not be able to produce good people. Corporately, you will not be able to produce good staff. You will get the staff that you deserve; if you are an unproductive leader, you will lead an unproductive staff. If you are a purpose driven leader you will lead a purpose driven staff. Once again, it's the law of attraction.

The Most High will hold you responsible for the people placed under your leadership, so be careful of what you do. How can you be a lead manager or supervisor if you don't know where you are going? Where are you taking your followers? Can the blind lead the blind?

You will find that many corporate leaders feel as if they cannot learn from you. They also feel as if you should not ask questions. Those that have the position of leadership and don't embrace questions should not lead because they only seek to control others. In addition, this is mental slavery because people have a right to question things they don't comprehend or things they need clarified; otherwise people are being subjected to blind faith. People who despise questions are dictators. You will always hear them say, "You ask too many questions." If you are working in an environment where you can't express yourself or be yourself, it is an unhealthy environment to be in.

Leaders competing with their staff

Some leaders are overly competitive in the workplace. Why should a mentor feel the need to compete with his/her mentee? This competitive spirit is the reason why most leaders fail. As a leader, you need to pass on as much information as you can to your mentee, not trying to hold on to your position and hide knowledge and information from them. Managers who feel as if they have to be so protective with their positions are not true leaders. True leaders understand that they have no competition. They comprehend that they are one of a kind, divine, unique and special. True leaders comprehend that they exist to discover new things, invent things, create ideas and leave it for the next generation so that those who come after them are guided on the right path. True leaders are happy when they develop other leaders. They are happy because they know that after they leave an area, the place can still function because they have left a proper system in place and they have given all that they had to offer.

True leaders understand that one day they will expire, so they implant their works into the hearts of people in order to live after they have expired. They comprehend the power of true influence.

True influence

The perception of influence is twisted. Many people get discouraged because people train them to pay attention to numbers (the amount of people who you influence). You will not survive the tactics of these systems if you care about popularity, or if your number one goal is acceptance, or if you are afraid to be rejected and criticized. You should not determine your effectiveness by numbers. You can have 20 people influenced by you, but those 20 people only amount to one person because they lack passion, determination, wisdom, persistence, etc. On the other hand, you may only influence one person, but that one person amounts to 20 people. They have the passion, determination, a positive mind-set, loyalty, commitment, etc. They have the ability to multiply, so which is more powerful? For this reason, I do not pay attention to numbers. If I have the ability to influence only one person in my life and they make positive changes, I am a person of influence indeed.

Lead by example

The best strategy of being a great leader is to lead by example. We don't see this too often from our leaders. Too many leaders want people to "do as they say" but not "do as they do." This is true hypocrisy. As a leader, remember that people mimic what they see. How can you as a supervisor be upset with your staff for taking long hours if you take long hours? How can you complain about your staff being unproductive if you're also unproductive? This is how people will lose respect for you. If you want to influence people positively, just live what you speak.

To lead by example is to have character. When you have character, you are a person that is guided by precepts, ethics, standards, laws, etc. that are not changeable by man or woman. In addition, you stand firm on what you believe in; you say things that you live and you live what you say. To lead by example means to stand out and to make sure that your private life is in alignment with your public life, not to live a life of contradiction. It is important to comprehend that this doesn't mean that as a leader you can't have a change of heart and that because you declared something it has to stay that way. If you have a change of heart because it is right, then as a true leader, declare your new decisions so that you can remain a person who is consistent and clear.

CHAPTER 13

Building a Family Empire

The transfer of wealth is very powerful, and it is a great method to ensure financial liberation and independence for future generations. Most wealthy people that exist today inherited their wealth. There are some people that exist such as celebrities and entrepreneurs that have started from humble beginnings and became very wealthy, but this isn't the norm for the common man and woman. They are once in a lifetime opportunities. Acquiring wealth is a journey; it doesn't build overnight, and it takes time and requires collective effort. A lot of less fortunate families can't afford the necessities of life, so certainly they are unable to provide great opportunities for their children, opportunities that will attract wealth to them.

There are certain privileges money and wealth will afford you. This is how the world works; there's no getting around it. Money answers all things, and you should want to make sure that your family has enough of it so that they don't become slaves to others. The achievement of wealth may seem impossible for the less fortunate, but it is very possible with financial strategies. People are not poor because they truly want to be. People live in poverty because they lack self-love, self-confidence and knowledge of self. The desire of all hearts is to live in abundance. If people knew who they really were and their potential, they would be in a better position to rise above these systems of oppression. Most people experience poverty because they come into a world that is designed to keep them in captivity, and they stay under captivity because they won't reform their mentality to gain liberation. The best method of ensuring that your children don't become economic slaves is to train them about themselves. Talk to them about their ancestors, where they came from and the importance of being free. You (the parent) must reveal their greatness. Your children won't have a great future if they're unaware of their past. Their future is connected to their past. The past will help them to comprehend who and what they are. Avoid those that want you to forget your past. You are who you are because of your past. You must know where you came from in order to know where you're going; otherwise your sense of direction will be flawed.

Children must be trained about financial wealth from tender ages. They must comprehend what it means to be a consumer and what it means to be a producer. Children have to be taught the value of money. Too many children learn bad spending habits; they are exposed frequently to the concept of consumption, so much so, that producing to them is a fantasy or for the rich. We need more parents to teach their children about production of goods.

Research shows that most people who start off working in family businesses become inspired to start a business of their own. The reason being is because when you grow up in this environment, it gives you a high sense of dignity and introduces you to a life that has meaning. Children will want to preserve their family legacy by having a standard that will make their parents proud. So if you want your children to have financial freedom and liberation to strengthen your lineage, be that example. When you have a successful family business, the chances of your children working for others are very small. It's a beautiful thing when you could have a job because you want to and not because you have too. When your employer talks down to you and belittles you, it's a beautiful thing to be able to stand your ground because you don't need their income, and if they fire you, you have a family business to depend on. This is how we strengthen generations; we must re-train them and take the job concept away from their mentality. Our children must be taught about the pride and dignity that comes along with ownership. We must drill into their minds that they have options. In addition, we must stop training them mentally that going to college is the route of success, when business is the true route. Businesses create wealth for families. When you go to college and obtain your degree, can you pass that degree on to your children when you expire? What happens to the degree when you expire? That degree becomes null and void. It has no power for your generation. It is a personal achievement. People need to get to the point where they reach towards family achievements. Businesses are family achievements.

Financial liberation and independence

Financial liberation and independence is not as hard as people think. It's just not for lazy and slothful people. You must be built to fight for the accomplishment of independence and liberation. The passion has to come from within. People run away from it because they don't want to put in the required effort; they would rather settle for the consistency of a salary. People have been brainwashed into thinking that it is hard. Oppressors would make you believe that to go into business is to lose and to have a job means to win. However, this concept is in reverse. We see the truth of this manifesting every day. The most people get out of jobs is a dependent income, status and title. The sky can be the limit on a job, but in entrepreneurship, the sky can be the floor or the starting ground.

Family Empires

Research also shows that a family business is the oldest form of business organization, with results that have been proven successful. Some successful family businesses are Wal-Mart, Nike, Volkswagen, Samsung Electronics, and Gucci. There are different types of family businesses such as an extended family business and an intimate family business, which is made up of a husband, wife and their children. An intimate family business is worth more than money/currency.

Advantages of having a family business

An intimate family business provides great advantages such as freedom, independence, control, flexibility, higher self-confidence, prestige and creativity. Because of the intimate relationship, parents will be able to distribute responsibilities based on soft skills (interests) and hard skills (technical). This gives the family an opportunity to highlight strengths and also to improve weaknesses. This is a method that gives the family businesses advantage over their competitors because they are maximizing each other's potentials. Businesses that are not family oriented hire employees that they don't know and they have to discover their staff's potencies, gifts, talents, values, etc., and this puts them at a disadvantage. It is time consuming. Time is valuable. In a family business, your co-workers are your family; you know them and you know how to interact with them. You won't have to worry about unforeseen character or personality traits that will damage the reputation of the company. In a family business, your co-workers, who are your family, genuinely care about you and they will be compassionate towards you, something that is so hard to get from co-workers that are not your family. It is very hard working around people that don't comprehend you and working around people that don't favor you. When you work around people you are comfortable with, it sets a great mood in the working environment. It will be relaxing, and your potential will flow effortlessly.

There are some disadvantages of having a family business: circumstances such as family conflicts, limited innovation, lack of a proper system, challenge with leadership succession and so forth. However, these challenges can be controlled by the matriarch of the family through training and discipline. These possible disadvantages cannot measure up to the long time rewards of having a family empire.

For me, the number one advantage of a family business is that it can be passed on through generations. If you desire to have a generational business (which is the ultimate goal), you should know that it requires a lot of hard work and discipline. Some family businesses don't survive because they don't generate enough wealth to transfer to the next generation. In order to survive, families must have strong financial skills, adapt the out of the box mentality, and be creative in order to continuously evolve.

Building a family empire will ensure parents that their children are not mistreated, enslaved and limited on jobs. Parents that build family empires are in the position to hire their own children, nurture them and teach them the self-reliance mentality. When you are employed by others, you have no leverage; you can't help your children when they need something to do as you choose to, because you are not in charge. Why should our children have to plead to be employed by others when we have the ability to provide work for them?

Implementing a family business strategy will cause your children to love and respect you more because they notice how you dedicate your life for their prosperity and success.

When you ask a child who their idol or hero is, often, it is an individual that they probably admire on television or in the community. Why can't parents always be listed as their children's number-one hero or idol? As a matter of fact, parents are earthly gods to their children, but many children don't see their parents as earthly gods because they didn't get the support and love they needed from their parents. If you want your children to be proud that they carry your DNA, do things that will truly benefit them. You must be an extraordinary parent and avoid parental mediocrity.

Energy is absorbed

The mind absorbs energy from other minds. Everything that exists is the source of energy; it can be given and it can be absorbed. Whoever your children spend more time with, they will absorb energy from. So if they go into the corporate plantation the moment they come out of high school, they will absorb the job mentality. As a parent, you have a wealth of knowledge and wisdom. You must share this power with your children. In addition, your children have creative abilities that you don't have, so when you come together in minds, your power will be mighty. Have you ever tried doing something and not been able to get it done and your child comes there and gets it done? This is new energy; why would you allow that energy to make someone else rich?

Parents and children need to bond more. Bonding happens when families work together. How awesome is it to be doing something that you truly love and have your children/ spouse in the next room helping you to accomplish goals that will empower them? There is nothing greater than doing something that you love, accomplishing wealth from it and being able to spend time with the people that you love the most!

When you decide to build an empire from your true work, your family (spouse, children) will put in their best efforts because they are stockholders.

They are part owners, and because they will benefit from this empire, they will make great investments into it. As stockholders they are free to make contributions and, particularly for your children, they will feel a high sense of importance because they are a part of something valuable. This will boost their self-esteem greatly, and they will feel a high sense of worth. Their support will be genuine, and you know that they have your best interests at heart. As I stated earlier, there are incalculable high potencies within your family bloodline, and so you must use wisdom and allow them to build your empire and not use their potencies for the benefit of others.

Keep it all in the family

Study the ants, this is how they operate: they don't separate themselves when it comes to achieving something; they work together, and unity and hard work is a key to their success. Families need to use the concept of the ants. If they come together, they will truly have something worth living for, and this is the height of joy and fulfilment. Many people fail because of the lack of support. They have a weak support system. There is no one in this world that is willing to support you more than your spouse (if you have one) and your children. Your family sincerely loves you and they will support you unequivocally. Why not involve them in your work? They will be loyal to you, and if you can't trust your own spouse and children, then who on earth can you trust?

Money Management

When you are trying to accomplish a goal that will benefit your lineage, splurging and spending unnecessary money must be avoided. Also, you must train your children to have the same mindset. You must comprehend that certain holidays and seasons were designed to keep you in poverty. If you're already behind in regards to wealth and you find yourself constantly having to spend the little that you have to celebrate money sucking holidays and seasons, how will you ever experience financial freedom and independence? If you want to gain economic power as a family, you must avoid contributing to each other's poverty. People must learn how to encourage their family members to save and invest. Think generational.

You must spend your finances on things that have real value: things such as real property. Have you ever wondered why they call it *real* property? Well, some properties are false; properties such as cars, fancy clothes, shoes, cell phones, flat-screen televisions, fancy furniture, etc. Truthfully, even money or currency have no true value. Wealth is bigger than currency. Money is only the means to obtain wealth. Money can be lost or lose value; however, wealth has the ability to last through generations; the value on it appreciates; it doesn't depreciate. When you have currency in abundance, you should exchange it for things that will outlive it: land, natural resources, gold, etc.

Statistics shows that the less fortunate spend more money on items that are non-transferable. They have the latest phones, they are up to date with fashion and they drive the best cars, but they die broke and most times their children have to borrow funds from the bank or other people to bury them when they die. This is insane. Instead of passing on benefits they pass on bills.

Those that are far behind in wealth need to be more strategic in financial planning in order to catch up with wealth. The fact that you are not wealthy means that you didn't have that financial support system like other families; this means less spending, increasing saving and intelligent investments.

Financial knowledge is power

When you have financial knowledge, you are dangerous to those who desire to oppress you because you have the ability to reach their level and have influence. This is why every family should seek to get intimately close with the financial system. You must know how to obtain and manage your finances so that you can be economically strong. People rarely listen to those who are less fortunate because they don't value them. Why? Well, humans are visual beings. They need to see that you're achieving success before they believe that you can help them achieve success. So if you want to influence people with your gift, you need wealth.

Don't expect people to give you wealth

Many people see politicians as their saviors. They often believe that politicians will make life better for them, despite the laws and policies put in place by the same politicians to further oppress them. Politicians' ultimate goal is not to make life better for you. They love power, so you shouldn't put the wealth of your generation in their hands. If you want to accomplish true wealth, you and your family must create your unique opportunities. When you are in a position to solve a problem or a need, you will always succeed.

Too many people are caught up in the lies and delusions of politicians, putting faith in parties, hoping for a brighter tomorrow that never come—not only politicians, others such as extended family members, friends, employers, etc. Too often, we look outside rather than within. People are too lazy to create their own wealth, so they become dependent on others for help when they have the power to do it themselves.

Life Insurance Policies

What is the goal of insurance? Insurance is a tool offered to consumers to manage risks. One thing that you can be certain of in life is that you will die/expire. It is very risky to go through life not practicing risk management.

Do you comprehend the benefit of having life insurance? There was a time when I didn't see it as important; I perceived insurance policies as a rip off. I still believe that it shares in the evil of the financial system. Many people feel the same way; they don't see the benefit of having it because it benefits others (spouse, children). A lot of people tasted their first taste of wealth through insurance policies. Even though it doesn't benefit you (parents) it will benefit your child/children (family) greatly, and this is the goal. Too many parents leave debts for their children instead of leaving them in better financial positions. The goal is to find a good reliable insurance policy that has proven to be trustworthy so that you can be assured that your loves are justly paid when you have expired.

Will your children be proud of you?

When people talk about you, will your children be proud or will they be ashamed? What legacy will you leave behind? Will they be able to boast about you, be proud to be a part of your lineage or will they despise you? Your children will not allow you to live through them if their memories of you are painful; create good memories for your lineage. A lot of kids are so angry and frustrated because they have to work so hard to survive. Happiness and fulfilment is only a fantasy or dream for many children. This is not the will of The Most

High. We should enjoy life and live in abundance. For this reason, we must be financially prudent and think about our children and ensure that every decision that is made will affect them for the greater good.

Many of the young adults feel as they don't have anything to live for; they never get the chance to taste wealth because of the way systems are designed. Many have given up on life. They are confused when it comes to their life's purpose and direction because they lack proper guidance and support from their parents. So they end up moving from job to job and nothing seems to be working out for them. They have rent or mortgage to pay, food costs, utility bills, taxes from the government, insurance, healthcare and recreational activities. Life is costly. Of all these things mentioned, housing is the critical one that eats up a lot of monies earned. This is why land is so important because if parents own enough land, that can be distributed to their children. When they don't have to put themselves in debt to buy land, it helps greatly. This is not about breeding lazy children, to think that shows that you have a slave mentality; it is about economic power and the preservation of one's race. The way some parents act towards their children depicts unconscious animosity. Love will make you protect the people that you love and it would cause you to want and provide the best that you can for them. Make your case known to your children; they must know that you are not in the business of charity. You will not just give them money; they have to earn the wealth. They have to make contributions towards the wealth.

Look around: the families that dominated the wealth generations ago do so today. They have been wealthy through generations because they believe in the philosophy of inheritance. How is it that a minority of earth's population is wealthy, probably 10 percent?

The Family Curse

When poverty is transferred through generations, it is often referred to as a family curse. The curse of poverty continues from generation to generation because no one in the generation wants to change anything. Hence, it doesn't have to be this way. Stop complaining about your parents faults and do what you think they should have done. Turn your parents' weaknesses into strengths. Treat your children better than you were treated. Be better and break the bad habits and the family curses. If you continue with the same negative family traditions, then you are not worthy to speak on the family curses because you aren't contributing to the family blessings. Every family bloodline has a redeemer. You're not reading this book by coincidence; you attracted this book to you. You have a responsibility to break the family curses. You are to be that beacon of light and the hope for your family. In actuality, every new generation should be better than the previous generation. This means that children should do greater works and be more successful than their parents. When children do greater works and accomplish more success than their parents, it shows progress in the family. If your parents were able to obtain a house, how is it that you don't have one? You should have something better than them or more houses and land than they had. What we see now is regress. There is no growth and development in regards to the family. When the mentee has less success than the mentor, it is safe to say that the mentor was ineffective and unproductive. The Messiah told his disciples that they would do greater works than him when he is gone.

So ask yourself, what wealth do you have in your possession for the empowerment of your children? Many parents are ignorant of their role and duty. They don't feel as if they should take responsibility for their children's lack of success. However, you are responsible, and this is why you shouldn't have children because you can, you should reproduce sensibly because you will be held accountable for your slothfulness by The Most High. A night of pleasure results in a never-ending nightmare or a life of trouble for many children. Your children are not mistakes; they are solutions and they are your future.

You are responsible for your children from the moment of conception in the womb to the tomb, not when they reach eighteen you give up responsibility. You are actually responsible for all your descendants. You are completely responsible for their performance, which is why you must put in the effort. Stop believing that your children should produce their own wealth without your financial, physical, emotional, and spiritual support. It's like you starting the race with the baton in your hand and, while running you drop the baton, so the next runner (generation) has no baton (wealth), so they can't continue the race; they are disqualified. The scriptures say that good parents leave an inheritance for their children. So if you don't have an inheritance to leave for your children, according to this scripture, you are not a good parent.

If you have five children, what good is it to have one house? Unfortunately, many parents find themselves in this position because this is the best that their salary allows them to do. A base salary could never allow an individual to have multiple homes and land; this is why it is a cage.

Parents that weren't fortunate enough to have an inheritance must use wisdom and only have the amount of children that they can comfortably afford to take care of. The more children you have, the greater the financial burden. This is why family planning is an important key because when you plan for something, you are expecting it to come forth and you will be prepared to handle it. Also, you should have children with a partner that shares your belief system and who will make sacrifices to empower your children.

You have to think bigger than a job. You have to think bigger to get bigger and do better to be better. We often say, "Oh that person has more money than he or she can spend in their lifetime." However, this is because that wealthy person is not thinking about their lifetime; they have obtained their wealth so that their bloodline can continue to dominate on earth.

> *Small-minded people think about what can benefit them in their lifetime. People that think big think about how their wealth will impact generations*

The concept of inheritance must be valued and acted upon, especially amongst those that have been subjugated by the lifestyle of poverty. If it is too late to pass on inheritance due to your age or whatever reason, it is okay. You can regain your good parental status by mentoring your children; be a part of their transformation. Teach them your weaknesses so that it could become their strengths.

ABOUT THE AUTHOR

Author Sherique Dill is the eldest daughter of her parents Cyril and Linda Simms of Murphy Town, Abaco. She is a true island girl; she grew up in Murphy Town, Abaco and later moved to New Providence to attend college, where she obtained her degree in business management. She is not the ordinary. While growing up she was very attached to her grandparents and preferred to sit and listen to their words of wisdom more than anything else.

Dill was later mesmerized by her dark chocolate irresistible song bird Jowelle Dill (Solo), an international recording artist, her husband of eight years. Currently they have two wonderful sons Joden and Jyelle Dill.

Dill loves to write because she feels that through writing her creativity is at its highest level. She describes herself as being down to earth but very discreet and strong minded. She is an introvert. She is energized when she is alone. She appears to be shy in the beginning but when she becomes familiar with a personality her exuberance is unforgettable. She values lifetime relationships and try to avoid friendships that will lead to drama or become short lived. Dill loves travelling, she loves to sing, she loves to sew and she loves to read. Dill also loves knowledge and information about business and finance. She expresses that her favourite thing to watch is a cooking show called 'Chopped'.

Previous book published by the Author: Created to Stand Out, Not Fit in, Available at Amazon and Create space.

CONNECT WITH THE AUTHOR
www.facebook.com/AuthorDill/
charisnasimms.wixsite.com/authorsheriquedill

www.ingramcontent.com/pod-product-compliance
Lightning Source LLC
Chambersburg PA
CBHW051315220526
45468CB00004B/1355